W9-CAA-426

OPPOSING
VIEWPOINTS®
SERIES

Doomsday Scenarios

Other Books of Related Interest:

Opposing Viewpoints Series

The Catholic Church

Church and State

Extremism

Pacifism

At Issue Series

Are Natural Disasters Increasing?

How Does Religion Influence Politics?

The Right to Die

What Is Humanity's Greatest Challenge?

Current Controversies Series

Assisted Suicide

The Elderly

Global Impact of Social Media

DISCARD

"Congress shall make no law ... abridging the freedom of speech, or of the press."

First Amendment to the US Constitution

The basic foundation of our democracy is the First Amendment guarantee of freedom of expression. The Opposing Viewpoints series is dedicated to the concept of this basic freedom and the idea that it is more important to practice it than to enshrine it.

OPPOSING VIEWPOINTS® SERIES

Doomsday Scenarios

Noah Berlatsky, Book Editor

GREENHAVEN PRESS

A part of Gale, Cengage Learning

GALE
CENGAGE Learning™

Detroit • New York • San Francisco • New Haven, Conn • Waterville, Maine • London

Christine Nasso, *Publisher*
Elizabeth Des Chenes, *Managing Editor*

© 2011 Greenhaven Press, a part of Gale, Cengage Learning

Gale and Greenhaven Press are registered trademarks used herein under license.

For more information, contact:
Greenhaven Press
27500 Drake Rd.
Farmington Hills, MI 48331-3535
Or you can visit our Internet site at gale.cengage.com

ALL RIGHTS RESERVED.
No part of this work covered by the copyright herein may be reproduced, transmitted, stored, or used in any form or by any means graphic, electronic, or mechanical, including but not limited to photocopying, recording, scanning, digitizing, taping, Web distribution, information networks, or information storage and retrieval systems, except as permitted under Section 107 or 108 of the 1976 United States Copyright Act, without the prior written permission of the publisher.

For product information and technology assistance, contact us at

Gale Customer Support, 1-800-877-4253
For permission to use material from this text or product, submit all requests online at www.cengage.com/permissions

Further permissions questions can be emailed to permissionrequest@cengage.com

Articles in Greenhaven Press anthologies are often edited for length to meet page requirements. In addition, original titles of these works are changed to clearly present the main thesis and to explicitly indicate the author's opinion. Every effort is made to ensure that Greenhaven Press accurately reflects the original intent of the authors. Every effort has been made to trace the owners of copyrighted material.

Cover image copyright © Ocean/Corbis.

LIBRARY OF CONGRESS CATALOGING-IN-PUBLICATION DATA

Doomsday scenarios / Noah Berlatsky, book editor.
    p. cm. -- (Opposing viewpoints)
  Includes bibliographical references and index.
    ISBN 978-0-7377-5721-7 (hardcover) -- ISBN 978-0-7377-5722-4 (pbk.)
  1. Parapsychology. 2. Prophecies. 3. End of the world. I. Berlatsky, Noah.
  BF1031.D665 2011
  001.9--dc22

                                                 2011000940

Printed in the United States of America
1 2 3 4 5 6 7 15 14 13 12 11

ACC LIBRARY SERVICES
AUSTIN, TX

Contents

Chapter 2: What Are Some Conflicts Involving Religious Doomsday Scenarios?

Chapter 3: How Might Humans Bring About Doomsday?

Why Consider Opposing Viewpoints?

> *"The only way in which a human being can make some approach to knowing the whole of a subject is by hearing what can be said about it by persons of every variety of opinion and studying all modes in which it can be looked at by every character of mind. No wise man ever acquired his wisdom in any mode but this."*
>
> John Stuart Mill

In our media-intensive culture it is not difficult to find differing opinions. Thousands of newspapers and magazines and dozens of radio and television talk shows resound with differing points of view. The difficulty lies in deciding which opinion to agree with and which "experts" seem the most credible. The more inundated we become with differing opinions and claims, the more essential it is to hone critical reading and thinking skills to evaluate these ideas. Opposing Viewpoints books address this problem directly by presenting stimulating debates that can be used to enhance and teach these skills. The varied opinions contained in each book examine many different aspects of a single issue. While examining these conveniently edited opposing views, readers can develop critical thinking skills such as the ability to compare and contrast authors' credibility, facts, argumentation styles, use of persuasive techniques, and other stylistic tools. In short, the Opposing Viewpoints Series is an ideal way to attain the higher-level thinking and reading skills so essential in a culture of diverse and contradictory opinions.

In addition to providing a tool for critical thinking, Opposing Viewpoints books challenge readers to question their own strongly held opinions and assumptions. Most people form their opinions on the basis of upbringing, peer pressure, and personal, cultural, or professional bias. By reading carefully balanced opposing views, readers must directly confront new ideas as well as the opinions of those with whom they disagree. This is not to argue simplistically that everyone who reads opposing views will—or should—change his or her opinion. Instead, the series enhances readers' understanding of their own views by encouraging confrontation with opposing ideas. Careful examination of others' views can lead to the readers' understanding of the logical inconsistencies in their own opinions, perspective on why they hold an opinion, and the consideration of the possibility that their opinion requires further evaluation.

Evaluating Other Opinions

To ensure that this type of examination occurs, Opposing Viewpoints books present all types of opinions. Prominent spokespeople on different sides of each issue as well as well-known professionals from many disciplines challenge the reader. An additional goal of the series is to provide a forum for other, less known, or even unpopular viewpoints. The opinion of an ordinary person who has had to make the decision to cut off life support from a terminally ill relative, for example, may be just as valuable and provide just as much insight as a medical ethicist's professional opinion. The editors have two additional purposes in including these less known views. One, the editors encourage readers to respect others' opinions—even when not enhanced by professional credibility. It is only by reading or listening to and objectively evaluating others' ideas that one can determine whether they are worthy of consideration. Two, the inclusion of such viewpoints encourages the important critical thinking skill of objectively evaluating an author's credentials and bias. This evaluation will illuminate an author's reasons for taking a particular stance on an issue and will aid in readers' evaluation of the author's ideas.

It is our hope that these books will give readers a deeper understanding of the issues debated and an appreciation of the complexity of even seemingly simple issues when good and honest people disagree. This awareness is particularly important in a democratic society such as ours in which people enter into public debate to determine the common good. Those with whom one disagrees should not be regarded as enemies but rather as people whose views deserve careful examination and may shed light on one's own.

Thomas Jefferson once said that "difference of opinion leads to inquiry, and inquiry to truth." Jefferson, a broadly educated man, argued that "if a nation expects to be ignorant and free ... it expects what never was and never will be." As individuals and as a nation, it is imperative that we consider the opinions of others and examine them with skill and discernment. The Opposing Viewpoints Series is intended to help readers achieve this goal.

David L. Bender and Bruno Leone,
Founders

Introduction

"We need to know about them [asteroids heading towards earth], and at the same time we need to be developing the technology (to divert one), and somebody needs to be in charge."

—*Former astronaut Russell Schweickart,* *quoted by Bruce Lieberman,* The Paramus Post, *November 3, 2010.*

Scientists believe that asteroids colliding with the earth have had a major impact on life on the planet. For example, an extensive scientific review of available evidence suggests that "The Cretaceous-Tertiary mass extinction which wiped out the dinosaurs and more than half of species on Earth, was caused by an asteroid colliding with Earth," according to a March 4, 2010, article on ScienceDaily.com. The asteroid in question is believed to have struck Mexico, and to have hit earth with a force more than a billion times more powerful than an atomic blast. The strike threw dust and ash into the atmosphere, blocking the sun and plunging all of earth into an unnatural winter. Scientists believe that the devastation and climate change were so traumatic that much of the life on earth died only a few days after impact.

The asteroid that scientists believe wiped out the dinosaurs hit earth around 70 million years ago. Since then, scientists think, there have been no comparable impact events. This may be quite unusual according to some scientists, who believe that for most of the history of earth, asteroid impacts occurred about once every 1 million years. "If this figure is correct, it would mean that intelligent life on Earth has developed only because of the lucky chance that there have been no major collisions in the past 70 million years," according to a January 7, 2010, article on DailyGalaxy.com.

The same DailyGalaxy.com article quotes Nick Bailey of the University of Southampton, who argues that "The threat of the Earth being hit by an asteroid is increasingly being accepted as the single greatest natural disaster hazard faced by humanity." Some scientists argue that the threat from asteroids is serious enough that the world should take steps to prevent a collision. What those steps should be, however, has caused some debate. Brent William Barbee of Emergent Space Technologies, Inc., argues that nuclear weapons could be used to divert the course of an asteroid. On the other hand, Piet Hut of Princeton University wants to use "a robotic tugboat that could attach itself to an asteroid to push it out of the Earth's path," according to Alok Jha writing on March 7, 2007, in the *Guardian*. A third idea would be to actually ram an asteroid with a ship: "The technology exists that would effectively allow scientists to send a craft into space to rear-end an asteroid, and slightly change its velocity," Melissa Eddy notes in an October 29, 2010, Associated Press article.

Eddy also writes that whatever option is chosen, any effort to change an asteroid's path "would require the approval of many nations," as well as a major investment of money and resources. For that reason, Thomas D. Jones of the National Aeronautics and Space Administration (NASA) gave a 2010 speech at the European Space Agency's operational center in which, according to Eddy, he made the case that any solution to the asteroid problem must involve "crossing international borders."

Other scientists have noted that the concern with the possibility of spectacular impact events can often be exaggerated in news reports. In a March/April 2005 article in the *Skeptical Inquirer*, NASA scientist David Morrison acknowledges that "Although the probabilities [of a meteor strike on earth] are low, a devastating impact capable of killing hundreds of millions of people could happen at any time." He also argues, however, that public discussion of meteors is often confused or misleading. For instance, he notes that "A common assertion in the tabloid press and on some Web sites is that we are at great risk from impacts, because impacts happen much more frequently than the scientists claim. Usually the argument is related to supposed evidence for recent large impacts." Morrison concludes that there is little evidence for such an increase in impact frequency and advises "a skeptical attitude" when approaching sensational stories.

Benny Peiser, a social anthropologist at John Moores University, also noted that fear of impact events has grown out of proportion to the real danger. "'Most people are simply not aware that we are making enormous progress in finding and identifying the population of Near Earth Objects [that is, of asteroids close to earth], and that the impact risk is thus diminishing year by year,' Peiser said," according to Andrea Thompson writing in an September 7, 2007, Livescience.com article. Bruce Koehn, a research scientist at Lowell Observatory, added, "The risk [of a major asteroid impact] is quite small. . . . It was never anything to lose sleep about, but it's even less now," as quoted in a July 23, 2010, article by Robert Lamb on Discovery News.

The following viewpoints look at other doomsday scenarios in chapters titled: Should Time-Specific Doomsday Predictions Be Taken Seriously? What Are Some Conflicts Involving Religious Doomsday Scenarios? and How Might Humans Bring About Doomsday? In each chapter, authors present different viewpoints as to how the earth or society may be endangered, how serious the threats are, and what should be done in response.

OPPOSING
VIEWPOINTS®
SERIES

CHAPTER 1

Should Time-Specific Doomsday Predictions Be Taken Seriously?

Chapter Preface

Nostradamus was a French doctor, astrologist, and occult scientist in the 1500s. He is known for a series of predictions, many focusing on catastrophes and doomsday scenarios. His predictions were published in a 10-part series called *Les Propheties* or *The Prophecies*, which consisted of cryptic rhyming four-line poems (or quatrains), written in a number of languages and codes.

Nostradamus achieved fame in his own day; one of his quatrains was thought to have predicted the death of King Henry II of France in a jousting accident. However, "Nostradamus' fame has only increased since his death," according to a November 2009 article on History.com. The article adds that Nostradamus' advocates "claim he had true prophetic powers and foretold a long list of world events, including the French Revolution, the Great Fire of London, World War I, the deaths of President John F. Kennedy and Princess Diana, and the US space shuttle Challenger disaster."

For example, one Nostradamus quatrain reads in translation:

"The blood of the just will commit
a fault at London,
Burnt through lighting of twenty
threes the six:
The ancient lady will fall from her
high place,
Several of the same sect will be
killed."

This is sometimes interpreted to have predicted the Great Fire of London in 1666. Medieval London is seen as "the ancient lady." In addition, "Only six deaths were recorded (hence 'the six' in the second line)" according to a Science Channel article online.

Critics, on the other hand, have argued that Nostradamus' predictions are too vague to be taken seriously. The same Science Channel article notes that "The doomsayers always warn that Nostradamus said the world was going to end," but despite various attempts at interpretation, no one is sure when exactly that end is supposed to occur. Robert T. Carroll writing in *The Skeptic's Dictionary* states that "Skeptics consider the 'prophecies' of Nostradamus to be mainly gibberish." Carroll points to one quatrain that claims that in 1999 a King of Terror will come from the sky to "resuscitate the great king of the Mongols." Some interpreters of Nostradamus claimed this prophecy might have been referring to the death in an airplane crash of John F. Kennedy, Jr., son of the former US President. Carroll argues that such an interpretation is obviously ridiculous.

Whether his prophecies are accurate or not, however, Nostradamus remains a very popular figure, and interest in his catastrophic prophecies remains high. The viewpoints that follow look at and evaluate other predictions involving doomsday scenarios.

> *"One thing the doomsday scenarios tend to share in common: They don't come to pass."*

Many Doomsday Prophecies Have Failed to Come to Pass

Benjamin Radford

Benjamin Radford is a science writer and the managing editor of the Skeptical Inquirer *and* Pensar. *In the following viewpoint, he discusses numerous end time prophecies. He starts by discussing a hen in Leeds in 1806 which laid eggs with "Christ is coming" written on them. He ends with minister Ronald Weinland, who declared in 2006 that the world would end within two years. Radford points out that none of these prophecies came true, and suggests that current doomsday predictions are unlikely to result in the end of the world either.*

As you read, consider the following questions:

1. According to the viewpoint, who was William Miller, and on what date did his followers claim the world would end?

2. What was Heaven's Gate, according to Radford?

Benjamin Radford, "10 Failed Doomsday Predictions," *LiveScience*, November 4, 2009. Copyright © 2009 TechMediaNetwork. All rights reserved. Reproduced by permission.

3. According to the author, what computer problem led some to believe that there would be massive computer failures in the year 2000?

With the upcoming disaster film "2012" [released in 2009] and the current hype about Mayan calendars[1] and doomsday predictions, it seems like a good time to put such notions in context.

Most prophets of doom come from a religious perspective, though the secular crowd has caused its share of scares as well. One thing the doomsday scenarios tend to share in common: They don't come to pass.

Here are 10 that didn't pan out, so far:

Doomsday, 1800s

The Prophet Hen of Leeds, 1806

History has countless examples of people who have proclaimed that the return of Jesus Christ is imminent, but perhaps there has never been a stranger messenger than a hen in the English town of Leeds in 1806. It seems that a hen began laying eggs on which the phrase "Christ is coming" was written. As news of this miracle spread, many people became convinced that doomsday was at hand—until a curious local actually watched the hen laying one of the prophetic eggs and discovered someone had hatched a hoax.

The Millerites, April 23, 1843

A New England farmer named William Miller, after several years of very careful study of his Bible, concluded that God's chosen time to destroy the world could be divined from a strict literal interpretation of scripture. As he explained to anyone who would listen, the world would end some time between March 21, 1843 and March 21, 1844. He preached and published enough to eventually lead thousands of followers

1. Based on interpretations of ancient Mayan calendars, some individuals have argued that the world will end in 2012.

(known as Millerites) who decided that the actual date was April 23, 1843. Many sold or gave away their possessions, assuming they would not be needed; though when April 23 arrived (but Jesus didn't) the group eventually disbanded—some of them forming what is now the Seventh Day Adventists.

Mormon Armageddon, 1891 or Earlier

Joseph Smith, founder of the Mormon church, called a meeting of his church leaders in February 1835 to tell them that he had spoken to God recently, and during their conversation he learned that Jesus would return within the next 56 years, after which the End Times would begin promptly.

Comets and Televangelists

Halley's Comet, 1910

In 1881, an astronomer discovered through spectral analysis that comet tails include a deadly gas called cyanogen (related, as the name imples, to cyanide). This was of only passing interest until someone realized that Earth would pass through the tail of Halley's comet in 1910. Would everyone on the planet be bathed in deadly toxic gas? That was the speculation reprinted on the front pages of *The New York Times* and other newspapers, resulting in a widespread panic across the United States and abroad. Finally even-headed scientists explained that there was nothing to fear.

Pat Robertson, 1982

In May 1980, televangelist and Christian Coalition founder Pat Robertson startled and alarmed many when—contrary to Matthew 24:36 ("No one knows about that day or hour, not even the angels in heaven . . .") he informed his "700 Club" TV show audience around the world that he knew when the world would end. "I guarantee you by the end of 1982 there is going to be a judgment on the world," Robertson said.

Heaven's Gate, 1997

When comet Hale-Bopp appeared in 1997, rumors surfaced that an alien spacecraft was following the comet—cov-

Halley's Comet Hysteria

During the latter half of the 19th century astronomers had developed a tool that enabled them to analyze the light being reflected by comets. . . . One of the earliest discoveries was that comets contained cyanogen, a very poisonous gas.

As Halley's Comet approached the sun in 1910, astronomers announced that Earth would actually pass through the tail of this comet. . . . They assured everyone that our planet was safe and suggested the possibility of some spectacular sunsets. Meanwhile, the doomsayers latched onto a potential link: if comets contain a poisonous gas and if Earth is going to pass through the comet's tail, then the people of Earth were in serious danger. Numerous newspapers actually published this story. Astronomers countered by saying the material in the tail was so spread out that there could be no ill affects, but few newspapers published this accurate information. Interestingly, a minor panic arose in some cities and entrepreneurs took advantage of it. They sold "comet pills" which were said to counter the effects of the poisonous gas. The pills sold like crazy. On May 20, after Earth had passed through the tail, everyone who had taken the pills was still alive . . . but, then, so was everyone else.

Gary Wikronk,
"Comet Hysteria and the Millenium: A Commentary," n.d.
http://cometography.com.

ered up, of course, by NASA [National Aeronautics and Space Administration] and the astronomical community. Though the claim was refuted by astronomers (and could be refuted by anyone with a good telescope), the rumors were publicized on Art Bell's paranormal radio talk show "Coast to Coast AM." These claims inspired a San Diego UFO [unidentified flying object] cult named *Heaven's Gate* to conclude that the world would end soon. The world did indeed end for 39 of the cult members, who committed suicide on March 26, 1997.

Predictions for 1999 and After

Nostradamus, August 1999

The heavily obfuscated and metaphorical writings of Michel de Nostredame have intrigued people for over 400 years. His writings, the accuracy of which relies heavily upon very flexible interpretations, have been translated and re-translated in dozens of different versions. One of the most famous quatrains read, "The year 1999, seventh month / From the sky will come great king of terror." Many Nostradamus devotees grew concerned that this was the famed prognosticator's vision of Armageddon.

Y2K, January 1, 2000

As the last century drew to a close, many people grew concerned that computers might bring about doomsday. The problem, first noted in the early 1970s, was that many computers would not be able to tell the difference between 2000 and 1900 dates. No one was really sure what that would do, but many suggested catastrophic problems ranging from vast blackouts to nuclear holocaust. Gun sales jumped and survivalists prepared to live in bunkers, but the new millennium began with only a few glitches.

May 5, 2000

In case the Y2K [Year 2000] bug didn't do us in, global catastrophe was assured by Richard Noone, author of the 1997 book *5/5/2000 Ice: the Ultimate Disaster*. According to Noone, the Antarctic ice mass would be three miles thick by May 5, 2000—a date in which the planets would be aligned in the heavens, somehow resulting in a global icy death (or at least a lot of book sales). Perhaps global warming kept the ice age at bay.

God's Church Ministry, Fall 2008

According to God's Church minister Ronald Weinland, the end times are upon us—again. His 2006 book *2008: God's Final Witness* states that hundreds of millions of people will die, and by the end of 2006, "there will be a maximum time of two years remaining before the world will be plunged into the worst time of all human history. By the fall of 2008, the United States will have collapsed as a world power, and no longer exist as an independent nation." As the book notes, "Ronald Weinland places his reputation on the line as the end-time prophet of God."

| "Now that the millennium has passed, the expectations of a significant number of Americans did not materialize."

Year 2000 (Y2K) Doomsday Scenarios Were Proven False

B.A. Robinson

B.A. Robinson lives in Kingston, Ontario, and writes for the website ReligiousTolerance.org. In the following viewpoint, Robinson explains that ReligiousTolerance.org had made several predictions for the year 2000, many of which (such as minor computer failures) came true. However, Robinson argues, doomsday predictions for the year 2000 did not come true, despite the fact that there was significant public belief in them. Robinson concludes by noting that there have been few studies to determine how Christians and others dealt with the failure of the prophecies.

As you read, consider the following questions:

1. B.A. Robinson predicted that some religious leaders would try to explain why Jesus Christ did not come as expected in 2000. According to Robinson, did this prediction come to pass?

B.A. Robinson, "The Millenium," ReligiousTolerance.org, May 15, 2005. Copyright © 1996 to 2005 by Ontario Consultants on Religious Tolerance. Reproduced by permission.

2. A Yankelovich Partners poll found that what percentage of Americans believed that the second coming of Christ would occur around the year 2000?

3. According to a Princeton Research Associates poll, what percentage of adult Americans believe that the world will end with the battle of Armageddon?

On 1999-DEC-2, this author made seven predictions of significant developments at the start of the new millennium in North America. As of 2004-MAR, some prophecies came true; two predictions thankfully failed. We predicted:

Y2K Predictions

- *Thousands of computer programs will fail,* largely in small commercial establishments. This will cause an unknown degree of disruption to all sectors of the economy. This seems to have happened. CNN and other news sources reported on 2000-JAN-1 that there were no noticeable electric power interruptions, except those caused by weather which were unrelated to Y2K (the year 2000). Some computer failures have happened; but no overwhelming catastrophe occurred.

- *Millions of misunderstandings will occur* in the way in which we record dates, after the year 2000. For example, consider 01/02/03. Does it mean January 02, 2003 or 01 February, 2003 or 2001-Feb-03? All three notations are in common usage. Apparently, society coped.

- *None of the events described in the Bible* will happen in the year 2000. The rapture, war of Armageddon, second coming of Jesus Christ, appearance of the Antichrist, etc. will not occur. No such events occurred at midnight, Palestine time, on the evening of 1999-DEC-31 as many people predicted. None happened during the rest of the year 2000, or since, either.

- *Some religious leaders* will explain why Jesus Christ did not come as expected. They will say that God has delayed the end of the world so that more people will have a chance to convert to Christianity and be saved. We have heard two sermons on Christian radio stations to this effect. However, most clergy seem to be ignoring this topic.

- *The growth of minority religions* will be viewed by some Christians as the main cause for Christ's delay. They will class these faith groups as "the enemy." This has not happened. There have been numerous attacks on religious minorities by political figures, including President G. [George] W. Bush. Most have been attempts to terminate the religious freedom of Wiccans. But otherwise, there have just been the usual anti-cult and counter-cult activity against new religions. Whether animosity will increase in the future is an open question.

- *A serious backlash against minority religions* will start circa 2002 and intensify for the following few years. These will include groups such as Jehovah's Witnesses, New Agers, Satanists, members of the Unification Church, Wiccans and other Neopagans. Other more established religious minorities such as Buddhism, Hinduism, Islam, Judaism, etc. will suffer as well. This did not happen at the last time when large numbers of Christians anticipated Christ's return—the "great disappointment" of 1844. It did not happen this time either. . . .

Nothing Happened in 2000

For many centuries, people have been predicting the year, the month and sometimes the day when:

- A violent and sudden end would terminate all life on earth;

- Major social and political upheavals would occur around the world;

- The war of Armageddon would take place in the Middle East;

- God would pour horrendous wrath on most of humanity; and/or

- Christ would return in what is referred to as the *second coming*.

The prophesiers have almost always predicted that these horrendous events would happen in their own immediate future.

All of these predictions share one factor: *none have ever come true.*

The year 2000 came and passed—a year that some considered very special, simply because it contained three zeros. A lot of people predicted that major events of cosmic proportion would happen. But no massive events actually came to pass. There were the usual number of major earthquakes, civil disturbances, tornados, people of different religions trying to exterminate each other—but nothing of a cosmic or even world-wide nature.

B.A. Robinson,
"The Millenium and End-of-the-World Predictions,"
ReligiousTolerance.org, November 10, 2009.

What Did the Public Expect
at or near the Millennium?

Many Christians believed that one or more momentous events
will happen near the start of the year 2001—one year before
the start of the actual millennium. Among the events anticipated were the end of the world as we know it, the battle of
Armageddon between the forces of good and evil, the return
of Jesus Christ to earth, or the rapture—a miraculous event in
which saved Christians, both dead or alive, will rise into the
sky to meet Jesus. Some public opinion polls gave interesting
results of the widespread nature of these beliefs:

- A Yankelovich Partners poll for *Time*/CNN in 1993-
  APR-28/9 found that 20% of Americans agreed that
  " . . . the second coming of Jesus Christ will occur
  sometime around the year 2000." 49% answered no,
  and 31% didn't know.

- An Associated Press poll in 1997 found that 24% of
  adult American Christians believed that Jesus Christ
  will return to earth within their lifetime and initiate the
  events described in the book of Revelation in the
  Christian Scriptures.

- A *U.S. News & World Report* poll on 1997-NOV-14 to
  16 revealed that:

    66% of Americans say that they believed that Jesus
    Christ will return to earth some day. This was an
    increase from 61% in 1994.

- Princeton Research Associates conducted a poll of 755
  randomly selected adults, for *Newsweek* magazine's
  1999-NOV-1 issue. They found that:

    The following percentage of adults believed that the
    world will end with the battle of Armageddon as
    described in the Biblical book Revelation:

40% of American adults generally

45% of Christian adults

71% of Evangelical Protestants

28% of non-Evangelical Protestants

18% of Roman Catholics

Of those who believed that Armageddon will happen:

47% believe that the Antichrist is on earth now

45% believe that Jesus will return during their lifetime

15% believed that Jesus' return to earth will occur as early as the year 2000 CE. Of this group:

83% believed that the second coming will be preceded by natural disasters; 66% by epidemics; 62% by mayhem

95% felt that they must "get right with the Lord" now in the expectation that Christ will return

62% felt an obligation to proselytize—to convert non-Christians

68% expected to go to heaven

57% believed in the final judgment where people will be divided into two groups for transportation to heaven or hell

In 1999-OCT, the Pew Research Center released a study called "Americans Look to the 21st Century." They confirmed the Princeton poll, finding:

44% believed that Jesus will probably return during their lifetime

22% said that Jesus will definitely return before 2050 CE

44% believed that Jesus will probably not return during their lifetime

Nothing Happened

According to CNN.com:

> Richard Landes, director of the Center for Millennial Studies at Boston University said: *"Any time of radical and rapid change is a great candidate for apocalyptic expectations. The idea that modernity is a runaway juggernaut that's leading us ultimately to destruction and only God can save us from it is obviously a tremendous stimulant to the apocalyptic imagination, 2000 or not, and will continue to stimulate the apocalyptic imagination after the passage of 2000."*

> Few soothsayers, however, are reserving an exact date for the end. Some Christian ministers are making vague predictions of a cataclysm somewhere around the year 2000. Many leave their calendars blank, warning followers to be prepared "at any time."

> Landes says: *"Most organized religious groups—denominations, churches and so on—are going to stay away from formal apocalyptic expectations. But all Christians, all Jews and all Muslims have built into their religion the belief that at some point all these things are going to happen."*

Now that the millennium has passed, the expectations of a significant number of Americans did not materialize. One of the great mysteries of the millennium is how these folks coped with their momentous disappointment when the year 2000 rolled into 2001 which rolled into 2002 without any apocalyptic events. We have not seen the results of any studies on this topic.

> "The reason nothing bad happened was that so many people put so much hard work into it."

The Y2K Doomsday Scenario Was a Real Danger Narrowly Averted

Catherine Winter

Catherine Winter is an editor and producer at American Radio-Works. In the following viewpoint, she reports that the worries about a computer failure at the beginning of 2000 were justified. Winter presents interviews with experts who say that, without all the money spent on upgrades before the year 2000 (Y2K) changeover, there would have been massive computer failures. Thus, Winter concludes, the Y2K scare was not a hoax, but a serious problem that was fixed before it could cause a disaster.

As you read, consider the following questions:

1. According to Winter, how much did government and businesses spend to fix software before Y2K?

2. What computer failures did John Koskinen say actually occurred on Y2K?

Catherine Winter, "The Surprising Legacy of Y2K, Separating Hype from Reality," American Public Media's *American RadioWorks®*, January 2005. Copyright © (p) 2005 American Public Media. Used with permission. All rights reserved.

3. What does Ben Levi say would have been the benefits of a Y2K disaster?

Y2K [Year 2000] inspired songs and novels and disaster movies. There was even a Y2K cookbook with recipes for all that freeze-dried food you might have stockpiled. Now they're historical curiosities on e-Bay. But in the 1990s, Y2K was on everyone's mind.

Computer Disaster

News shows talked about the threat of a major computer malfunction that might hit in the year 2000.

On ABC News, Forrest Sawyer introduced a Y2K segment this way:

"Surf through the Internet these days and you keep coming across a strange word, TEOTWAWKI. It stands for 'the end of the world as we know it,' and it refers to the effects of a tiny, seemingly innocuous computer glitch, a tiny glitch a lot of people say could literally blow the lights out on civilization."

The glitch was this: in the early days of programming, computer code used two-digit numbers for dates, like '70' for 1970. That let computers work faster. No one thought the software would still be in use decades later, but it was. As the year 2000 approached, programmers started warning that computers could misread the '00' as the year 1900. That might cause breakdowns. No one knew how widespread computer malfunctions might be, but people started thinking about all the things that are run by computers.

Things like hospital equipment, air traffic control, and nuclear weapons.

Some Christians saw the Y2K bug as a fulfillment of Biblical prophecies about the end of the world.

"Could this be God's way to bring revival to America?" asked televangelist Jerry Falwell in a video called *A Christian's*

Guide to the Millennium Bug. "Stop and think about it: when water, food, electricity, gas, oil, money, none of them are available and nowhere to get them, the people who have those things will be in mortal danger of attack from those who don't have them."

Gun sales spiked. Doomsayers hawked things like gas masks and radiation kits. Worried people stashed batteries and food. The Federal Reserve pumped an extra $50 billion in cash into circulation in case people withdrew their savings. The U.S. government spent nearly $9 billion to fix its computers. Businesses spent many times more. All told, businesses and government spent more than a $100 billion to fix software.

And then, Friday night turned to Saturday morning, and the apocalypse was a no-show.

So what happened? Were we sold a bill of goods by people who could make a buck hyping Y2K? Was all the money we spent really necessary?

Not Hype

"This was not hype," says Paul Saffo, Director of the Institute for the Future in Menlo Park, California. "This was not software consultants trying to create a full employment act for themselves."

In the 90s, Saffo worked to persuade businesses that they would have to do something about the Y2K bug. "This really could have screwed up our lives, and you know, a whole bunch of little geeks saved us."

Saffo says some businesses under-reacted to the problem at first, and then spent more money than they should have scrambling to fix their software. But it did have to be fixed. Before Y2K hit, many businesses ran tests. They advanced their computer clocks to 2000 and the computers didn't work.

One of the programmers who worked on the fix was David Eddy. He's widely regarded as the guy who coined the term "Y2K." Eddy is still sore that people think there wasn't really a problem.

"I'd love to do a poll," says Eddy, "and eliminate anybody that actually worked on year 2000 work and just talk to, what I would call civilians, and if you ask them, I bet you hard money that most civilians would say, 'Oh, Y2K, whole thing was a hoax. Bodies didn't fall from the sky at the stroke of midnight, I knew the thing was a hoax.' But the reason nothing bad happened was that so many people put so much hard work into it."

Eddy would like a little gratitude for the people who raced to fix the Y2K bug, but doing a good job made them invisible. Just ask John Koskinen. He was appointed by President [Bill] Clinton to oversee Y2K fixes.

"The only way to be a hero," says Koskinen, "would be for half the world to stop and then somehow get it started again which was not one of our goals. Like a lot of things in government, if it works well nobody cares much."

Koskinen points to evidence that the fix was needed. Some computers that didn't get fixed stopped working on New Year's Day. He says some of those glitches would normally have been big news, but since people were expecting the end of the world, they didn't seem like that big a deal. Koskinen was in the Y2K nerve center in Washington, D.C. that night, monitoring systems all over the world. He says the public doesn't realize how many things went wrong.

Koskinen describes the scene as he saw it unfurl. "The low level wind shear detectors at every major airport go out at 7:00 on Friday night, the defense intelligence satellite system goes down, the French intelligence satellite goes down, the Japanese lose the ability to monitor a couple of their nuclear power plants, and come Monday morning, there are thousands of businesses that when you buy something with your credit card, charge you every day of the week."

But in the end, most major business and government computers did get fixed. In fact, so few things went wrong that after Y2K, some businesspeople complained that the money they spent was wasted. But *Business Week* chief economist Michael Mandel disagrees. He says Y2K forced business to make upgrades that they're still using.

"If you look at the Y2K," says Mandel, "you can sort of say, 'Maybe we didn't have to be so wired up about it.' But the fact is, it may have been the right thing to do from a social and economic point of view."

Still Prepared

Mandel worries that Y2K may have lured people into a false sense of security. Next time there's a big disaster looming, people may think it's just hype and ignore the warnings. But some people are still prepared for the end of the world as we know it.

Ben Levi built a house in the foothills of Boulder, Colorado designed to survive Y2K. It's a bright, airy place, with three computers in the office and a fountain trickling in the living room. And if the utilities had shut down on New Year's Day, Levi could have kept the computers humming and the fountain flowing with his solar panels and his generator.

"In a way," says Levi, "I was kind of looking forward to it. Wouldn't this be fun, because I really felt that I could meet the challenge."

Levi's not a survivalist; he's a computer consultant. He believed Y2K might be a real catastrophe. But the end of the world as we know it also offered an opportunity to build a better world.

"We would be coming more into balance," says Levi. "Less obsessed with technology and materialism. The opportunity was that it would basically turn the volume down on civilization for awhile."

But if anything, civilization is even noisier, more interconnected, more dependent on technology. So Levi figures, who
knows? A crisis could still happen, like the massive East Coast
power failure in 2003. And if it does, he's still got the year's
supply of dried food he stashed.

> "Up until this point, I firmly believed that the possibility of 2012 being catastrophic in some way was worth investigating. The report made it a little too real."

The 2012 Mayan Doomsday Scenario May Have a Scientific Basis

Lawrence Joseph, interviewed by Brandon Keim

Brandon Keim is a journalist and a writer for Wired.com. In the following viewpoint, he talks to Lawrence Joseph, an author who has written on 2012 doomsday scenarios. The two discuss the results of a recent National Aeronautics and Space Administration (NASA) study which suggests that solar storms in 2012 may have devastating effects on American and world power grids. Joseph argues that such storms could do billions of dollars in damage and shut down power grids worldwide. Joseph also speculates that the solar storms may be linked to the doomsday event predicted by the ancient Mayan calendar for the year 2012.

Brandon Keim and Lawrence Joseph, "The 2012 Apocalypse—And How to Stop It," Wired.com, April 17, 2009. Copyright © 2009 Condé Nast Publications. All rights reserved. Originally published in Wired.com. Reprinted by permission. http://www.wired.com/wiredscience/2009/04/2012storms/.

As you read, consider the following questions:

1. According to the viewpoint, NASA-assembled researchers argued that solar flares could unleash waves of energy that would result in what consequences?

2. According to Lawrence Joseph, the ancient Mayans saw 2012 not as the end of the world, but as what?

3. Joseph says that shutting the power grid off and restarting it would cost how much money?

For scary speculation about the end of civilization in 2012, people usually turn to followers of cryptic Mayan prophecy, not scientists. But that's exactly what a group of NASA [National Aeronautics and Space Administration]-assembled researchers described in a chilling report issued earlier this year [2009] on the destructive potential of solar storms.

2012 Solar Flares

Entitled "Severe Space Weather Events—Understanding Societal and Economic Impacts," it describes the consequences of solar flares unleashing waves of energy that could disrupt Earth's magnetic field, overwhelming high-voltage transformers with vast electrical currents and short-circuiting energy grids. Such a catastrophe would cost the United States "$1 trillion to $2 trillion in the first year," concluded the panel, and "full recovery could take 4 to 10 years." That would, of course, be just a fraction of global damages.

Good-bye, civilization.

Worse yet, the next period of intense solar activity is expected in 2012, and coincides with the presence of an unusually large hole in Earth's geomagnetic shield. But the report received relatively little attention, perhaps because of 2012's supernatural connotations. Mayan astronomers supposedly predicted that 2012 would mark the calamitous "birth of a new era."

Whether the Mayans were on to something, or this is all just a chilling coincidence, won't be known for several years. But according to Lawrence Joseph, author of *Apocalypse 2012: A Scientific Investigation into Civilization's End*, "I've been following this topic for almost five years, and it wasn't until the report came out that this really began to freak me out." . . .

The Power Grid Is Vulnerable

Wired.com: Do you think it's coincidence that the Mayans predicted apocalypse on the exact date when astronomers say the sun will next reach a period of maximum turbulence?

Lawrence Joseph: I have enormous respect for Mayan astronomers. It disinclines me to dismiss this as a coincidence. But I recommend people verify that the Mayans prophesied what people say they did. I went to Guatemala and spent a week with two Mayan shamans who spent 20 years talking to other shamans about the prophecies. They confirmed that the Maya do see 2012 as a great turning point. Not the end of the world, not the great off-switch in the sky, but the birth of the fifth age.

Isn't a great off-switch in the sky exactly what's described in the report?

The chair of the NASA workshop was Dan Baker at the Laboratory for Atmospheric and Space Physics. Some of his comments, and the comments he approved in the report, are very strong about the potential connection between coronal mass ejections [that is, a burst of solar wind released from the sun] and power grids here on Earth. There's a direct relationship between how technologically sophisticated a society is and how badly it could be hurt. That's the meta-message of the report.

I had the good fortune last week to meet with John Kappenman at MetaTech. He took me through a meticulous two-hour presentation about just how vulnerable the power grid is, and how it becomes more vulnerable as higher voltages are sent across it. He sees it as a big antenna for space weather outbursts.

Why is it so vulnerable?

Ultra-high voltage transformers become more finicky as energy demands are greater. Around 50 percent already can't handle the current they're designed for. A little extra current coming in at odd times can slip them over the edge.

The ultra-high voltage transformers, the 500,000- and 700,000-kilovolt transformers, are particularly vulnerable. The United States uses more of these than anyone else. China is trying to implement some million-kilovolt transformers, but I'm not sure they're online yet.

Kappenman also points out that when the transformers blow, they can't be fixed in the field. They often can't be fixed at all. Right now there's a one- to three-year lag time between placing an order and getting a new one.

According to Kappenman, there's an as-yet-untested plan for inserting ground resistors into the power grid. It makes the handling a little more complicated, but apparently isn't anything the operators can't handle. I'm not sure he'd say these could be in place by 2012, as it's difficult to establish standards, and utilities are generally regulated on a state-by-state basis. You'd have quite a legal thicket. But it still might be possible to get some measure of protection in by the next solar climax.

Preparing for Solar Storms

Why can't we just shut down the grid when we see a storm coming, and start it up again afterwards?

Power grid operators now rely on one satellite called ACE, which sits about a million miles out from Earth in what's called the gravity well, the balancing point between sun and earth. It was designed to run for five years. It's 11 years old, is losing steam, and there are no plans to replace it.

Space Weather and Power Grids

Modern society depends heavily on a variety of technologies that are susceptible to the extremes of space weather—severe disturbances of the upper atmosphere and of the near-Earth space environment that are driven by the magnetic activity of the Sun. Strong auroral currents can disrupt and damage modern electric power grids and may contribute to the corrosion of oil and gas pipelines. Magnetic storm-driven ionospheric density disturbances interfere with high-frequency (HF) radio communications and navigation signals from Global Positioning System (GPS) satellites, while polar cap absorption (PCA) events can degrade—and, during severe events, completely black out—HF communications along transpolar aviation routes, requiring aircraft flying these routes to be diverted to lower latitudes. Exposure of spacecraft to energetic particles during solar energetic particle events and radiation belt enhancements can cause temporary operational anomalies, damage critical electronics, degrade solar arrays, and blind optical systems such as imagers and star trackers.

The effects of space weather on modern technological systems are well documented in both the technical literature and popular accounts. Most often cited perhaps is the collapse within 90 seconds of northeastern Canada's Hydro-Quebec power grid during the great geomagnetic storm of March 1989, which left millions of people without electricity for up to 9 hours. This event exemplifies the dramatic impact that extreme space weather can have on a technology upon which modern society in all of its manifold and interconnected activities and functions critically depends.

Space Studies Board, Severe Space Weather Events—
Understanding Societal and Economic Impacts:
A Workshop Report, *2008. www.nap.edu.*

ACE provides about 15 to 45 minutes of heads-up to power plant operators if something's coming in. They can shunt loads, or shut different parts of the grid. But to just shut the grid off and restart it is a $10 billion proposition, and there is lots of resistance to doing so. Many times these storms hit at the north pole, and don't move south far enough to hit us. It's a difficult call to make, and false alarms really piss people off. Lots of money is lost and damage incurred. But in Kappenman's view, and in lots of others, this time burnt could really mean burnt.

Do you live your life differently now?

I've been following this topic for almost five years. It wasn't until the report came out that it began to freak me out.

Up until this point, I firmly believed that the possibility of 2012 being catastrophic in some way was worth investigating. The report made it a little too real. That document can't be ignored. And it was even written before the THEMIS [Time History of Events and Macroscale Interactions during Substorms] satellite discovered a gigantic hole in Earth's magnetic shield. Ten or twenty times more particles are coming through this crack than expected. And astronomers predict that the way the sun's polarity will flip in 2012 will make it point exactly the way we don't want it to in terms of evading Earth's magnetic field. It's an astonishingly bad set of coincidences.

If [President] Barack Obama said, "Lets' prepare," and there weren't any bureaucratic hurdles, could we still be ready in time?

I believe so. I'd ask the President to slipstream behind stimulus package funds already appropriated for smart grids, which are supposed to improve grid efficiency and help transfer high energies at peak times. There's a framework there. Working within that, you could carve out some money for the ground resistors program, if those tests work, and have the initial momentum for cutting through the red tape. It'd be a place to start.

> *"The basic misunderstanding . . . comes from a presumption that the Maya regarded calendars, dates, and deities the way Western culture does."*

The 2012 Mayan Doomsday Scenario Is Groundless

Craig Smith

Craig Smith is a writer for the Santa Fe New Mexican, *a daily newspaper published in Santa Fe, New Mexico. In the following viewpoint, Smith reports on the popular idea that the world will end in 2012 as predicted by the ancient Mayan calendar. He reports that expert Mark Van Stone, who has a doctorate in Latin American studies, believes that the idea of an apocalypse in 2012 has no basis in Mayan traditions. Stone believes the misunderstanding about 2012 comes from viewing Mayan calendars, dates, and deities the way Western culture views them. Ultimately, it is concluded that there is no reason to believe the world will end in 2012.*

As you read, consider the following questions:

    1. According to Stone, what do the "2012-ologists" have in common?

Craig Smith, "Apocalypse Not Yet (Pasatiempo)," *Santa Fe New Mexican*, May 30, 2008. Reprinted with permission.

2. Western time is linear. What, according to Stone, is Mayan time?

3. According to the viewpoint, how many calendars did the Maya use?

Humans can find signs of the world's impending destruction in anything, especially when religious beliefs are involved. Sunspots, comets, planetary lineups. Earthquakes, typhoons, hurricanes. Wars, price increases, Y2K [Year 2000]. You name it, someone has or will seize it as proof that the end is near.

Point out that no such prediction has ever borne its fatal fruit, and believers will do what Fanny Squeers [fictional character] did in [Charles] Dickens' *Nicholas Nickleby*: pity your ignorance and despise you. This time, they insist, it's really going to happen. Just you wait . . .

One recent goodbye-world movement is focused on Dec. 21, 2012, when the ancient Maya "Long Count" calendar supposedly ends. People are blogging, writing, and publishing about it to a fare-thee-well, for many believe it heralds a long-predicted cataclysm.

It's Not the End of the World

However, calligrapher, author, and hieroglyph expert Mark Van Stone is in no hurry to pack his bags, and he explains why in a lecture on Friday, May 30, [2008] at the New Mexico Museum of Art: "It's Not the End of the World: What the Ancient Maya Really Said About 2012."

"I've done a lot of reading of stuff put out by the 2012-ologists," said Stone, who has a doctorate in Latin American studies and teaches art history at Southwestern College in Chula Vista, California. "What they have in common is they have very rich imaginations and they project it onto these things. There are only a few of them who have a foot in the scientific world. Everyone else is woefully ignorant and maybe even willfully ignorant."

The basic misunderstanding, Stone said, comes from a presumption that the Maya regarded calendars, dates, and deities the way Western culture does. For example, Westerners mark time by counting days, months, and years using the base-10 system derived from our 10 fingers, and no year repeats—time is linear. The Maya counted in base 20 and believed in cyclical time. When their Long Count reset every several thousand years—when it reached 13,000 in base 20—it was just like an odometer clicking back to zero, Stone said. The occasion was a cause for festivities, not a portent of cataclysm. "They celebrated these years with pomp; there were jubilees."

They also had what Stone calls "impossible numbers"—dates that could literally never occur in their base-20 system but still appeared tied to events in writings or carvings. Perhaps they were the Mesoamerican version of a blue moon or the 12th of Never.

What about texts that supposedly predict cataclysms along with the year change? Stone laughed. "There is only one monument that has the 2012 date listed," he said. "Unfortunately, there is damage on it. It's incomplete. It states that at this time, the Maya god of change and transition . . . will descend to someplace—that part is broken—and do something unclear. But I don't think the Maya projected the end of the world.

"The Popol Vuh [Maya creation myth] tells of four creations. Each one is an improvement on the last. The first creation was animals, then the gods had a flood and wiped it all away and started over. They made people of clay, and they melted in the rain. They made people of wood, and they couldn't speak.

"In this current fourth creation, they made people of corn, maize, and then had to diminish their size and knowledge and power." There's nothing in the Maya documentation about this "fourth creation" that suggests the world will end when the calendar resets, said Stone.

The Maya used three calendars, Stone explained—the Long Count calendar, a 365-day solar calendar, and another built around a 260-day period.

"The most important calendar was Tzolk'in. K'in was the word for day, and tzol means 260. It was mainly divinatory; it had, apparently, some relationship with the natural cycle. But then, you see, it's immediately out of sync with the solar cycle.

"It is a multiple of 20 and 13, and those two numbers are very important to Maya culture. They went barefoot, and they counted on fingers and toes. The number 20 was called 'whole man.'

"From the time of planting to the time of harvesting corn is about 260 days, depending on latitude and altitude. The time from when a woman first misses her period to giving birth is 260 days, just under nine months. And at the latitude of 14 degrees, 8 minutes—two important Maya cities were on that latitude—the sun reaches zenith twice a year. They're 260 days apart."

Maya Writing

Stone prizes something else about the Maya: they viewed writing—even with errors—as dictated by higher powers. "The Maya scribes did something that, as far as I know, no one else did in the world. They didn't correct errors in writing. There are many arithmetical mistakes, or where they used the wrong glyph in writing, in books or on stone records.

"Nearly everything written down was ritually chanted at some point. If they were writing down words of a holy liturgy and somebody misspoke, they thought the gods did it. If a carver did something wrong, the gods meant it to happen. A card laid is a card played."

That mix of beauty and brashness captivates Stone. "I fell in love with Maya writing, because it's so different from other writing systems of the world. It's quite beautiful when done right and also has an allure of mystery. It's like finding a lost city. You walk into this new world."

Mistakes or not, Mayan public writing was meant to be beautiful. Scribes might write a three-glyph word with the glyphs packed together or separated, depending on how it looked. "Ancient writing done in public, Chinese or Egyptian or Mayan or Roman, was not meant to be read by nearly everybody," Stone stressed. "Only a few people could read then. But it had to look good. It had to impress people who couldn't read it. The visual power of beautiful calligraphy was very important."

Stone will begin his lecture by explaining the Maya calendar systems "as quickly and efficiently as possible. I'll lose the audience if I get into the math!" Then he intends to explain that "the Maya have left us very fragmentary evidence about what they believed, and they had very different ideas about how hard and fast a calendar date is." From there, he will deal with 2012 versus the 13,000 Long Count calendar date and its significance.

"The main point about the 2012-ologists is [that] they're imputing enormous precision and very Western mechanical leanings to the Mayas," he said. "They talk about galaxies lining up, about the solstice, the flipping of the Earth's magnetic field on that Dec. 21, blah, blah, blah.

"The Mayas calculated that day as being important, as a large multiple of sacred numbers. That's all."

> *"'The hands of the Clock of Doom have moved again,' the* Bulletin *announces. 'Only a few more swings of the pendulum, and, from Moscow to Chicago, atomic explosions will strike midnight for Western civilization.'"*

The Doomsday Clock Has Provided a Gauge of World Danger

Bulletin of the Atomic Scientists

The Bulletin of the Atomic Scientists *is an online magazine that covers issues related to the dangers of nuclear weapons and other man-made catastrophes. In the following viewpoint, the* Bulletin *provides a timeline of changes in their Doomsday Clock, from 1947 to 2010. The clock shows how much danger the* Bulletin *believes the world is in; the closer to midnight the clock is set, the closer the world is to destruction. The viewpoint explains the conditions which led the* Bulletin *to adjust the clock over time. It also notes that the clock is meant to convey the danger of nuclear war to both the public and politicians.*

Bulletin of the Atomic Scientists, "Timeline," 2010. Copyright © 2010 Bulletin of the Atomic Scientists. All rights reserved. Reproduced by permission of Bulletin of the Atomic Scientists: The Magazine of Global Security News & Analysis.

As you read, consider the following questions:

1. Between 2007 and 2010, how was the clock adjusted, and what reasons does the *Bulletin* give for this change?

2. According to the *Bulletin*, was 1984 a good year for arms control talks? Why or why not?

3. The Doomsday Clock was closer to midnight in 1953 than ever before or since. What dangerous events happened in that year, according to the *Bulletin*?

*I*t is 6 Minutes to Midnight[1], 2010: International cooperation rules the day. Talks between Washington and Moscow for a follow-on agreement to the Strategic Arms Reduction Treaty are nearly complete, and more negotiations for further reductions in the U.S. and Russian nuclear arsenal are already planned. Additionally, Barack Obama becomes the first U.S. president to publicly call for a nuclear-weapon-free world. The dangers posed by climate change are still great, but there are pockets of progress. Most notably: At Copenhagen [Denmark], the developing and industrialized countries agree to take responsibility for carbon emissions and to limit global temperature rise to 2 degrees Celsius.

Threat of Disaster in the 2000s

It is 5 Minutes to Midnight, 2007: The world stands at the brink of a second nuclear age. The United States and Russia remain ready to stage a nuclear attack within minutes, North Korea conducts a nuclear test, and many in the international community worry that Iran plans to acquire the Bomb. Climate change also presents a dire challenge to humanity. Dam-

---

1. "6 minutes to midnight" refers to the time on the Doomsday Clock. The clock is a clockface maintained since 1947 by the board of directors of the *Bulletin of the Atomic Scientists*. The clock is moved closer to midnight when the world is estimated to be closer to global disaster.

age to ecosystems is already taking place; flooding, destructive storms, increased drought, and polar ice melt are causing loss of life and property.

It is 7 Minutes to Midnight, 2002: Concerns regarding a nuclear terrorist attack underscore the enormous amount of unsecured—and sometimes unaccounted for—weapon-grade nuclear materials located throughout the world. Meanwhile, the United States expresses a desire to design new nuclear weapons, with an emphasis on those able to destroy hardened and deeply buried targets. It also rejects a series of arms control treaties and announces it will withdraw from the Anti-Ballistic Missile Treaty.

Threat of Disaster in the 1990s

It is 9 Minutes to Midnight, 1998: India and Pakistan stage nuclear weapons tests only three weeks apart. "The tests are a symptom of the failure of the international community to fully commit itself to control the spread of nuclear weapons—and to work toward substantial reductions in the numbers of these weapons," a dismayed *Bulletin* reports. Russia and the United States continue to serve as poor examples to the rest of the world. Together, they still maintain 7,000 warheads ready to fire at each other within 15 minutes.

It is 14 Minutes to Midnight, 1995: Hopes for a large post-Cold War peace dividend and a renouncing of nuclear weapons fade. Particularly in the United States, hard-liners seem reluctant to soften their rhetoric or actions, as they claim that a resurgent Russia could provide as much of a threat as the Soviet Union. Such talk slows the rollback in global nuclear forces; more than 40,000 nuclear weapons remain worldwide. There is also concern that terrorists could exploit poorly secured nuclear facilities in the former Soviet Union.

It is 17 Minutes to Midnight, 1991: With the Cold War officially over, the United States and Russia begin making deep cuts to their nuclear arsenals. The Strategic Arms Reduction

Treaty greatly reduces the number of strategic nuclear weapons deployed by the two former adversaries. Better still, a series of unilateral initiatives remove most of the intercontinental ballistic missiles and bombers in both countries from hair-trigger alert. "The illusion that tens of thousands of nuclear weapons are a guarantor of national security has been stripped away," the *Bulletin* declares.

It is 10 Minutes to Midnight, 1990: As one Eastern European country after another (Poland, Czechoslovakia, Hungary, Romania) frees itself from Soviet control, Soviet General Secretary Mikhail Gorbachev refuses to intervene, halting the ideological battle for Europe and significantly diminishing the risk of all-out nuclear war. In late 1989, the Berlin Wall [in Germany] falls, symbolically ending the Cold War. "Forty-four years after [British prime minister] Winston Churchill's 'Iron Curtain' speech, the myth of monolithic communism has been shattered for all to see," the *Bulletin* proclaims.

Threat of Disaster in the 1980s

It is 6 Minutes to Midnight, 1988: The United States and Soviet Union sign the historic Intermediate-Range Nuclear Forces Treaty, the first agreement to actually ban a whole category of nuclear weapons. The leadership shown by President Ronald Reagan and Soviet Premier Mikhail Gorbachev makes the treaty a reality, but public opposition to U.S. nuclear weapons in Western Europe inspires it. For years, such intermediate-range missiles had kept Western Europe in the crosshairs of the two superpowers.

It is 3 Minutes to Midnight, 1984: U.S.-Soviet relations reach their iciest point in decades. Dialogue between the two superpowers virtually stops. "Every channel of communications has been constricted or shut down; every form of contact has been attenuated or cut off. And arms control negotiations have been reduced to a species of propaganda," a concerned *Bulletin* informs readers. The United States seems to flout the few arms control agreements in place by seeking an expansive, space-based anti-ballistic missile capability, raising worries that a new arms race will begin.

It is 4 Minutes to Midnight, 1981: The Soviet invasion of Afghanistan hardens the U.S. nuclear posture. Before he leaves office, President Jimmy Carter pulls the United States from the Olympic Games in Moscow and considers ways in which the United States could win a nuclear war. The rhetoric only intensifies with the election of Ronald Reagan as president. Reagan scraps any talk of arms control and proposes that the best way to end the Cold War is for the United States to win it.

It is 7 Minutes to Midnight, 1980: Thirty-five years after the start of the nuclear age and after some promising disarmament gains, the United States and the Soviet Union still view nuclear weapons as an integral component of their national security. This stalled progress discourages the *Bulletin*: "[The Soviet Union and United States have] been behaving like what may best be described as 'nucleoholics'—drunks who continue to insist that the drink being consumed is positively 'the last one,' but who can always find a good excuse for 'just one more round.'"

Threat of Disaster in the 1970s and 1960s

It is 9 Minutes to Midnight, 1974: South Asia gets the Bomb, as India tests its first nuclear device. And any gains in previous arms control agreements seem like a mirage. The United States and Soviet Union appear to be modernizing their nuclear forces, not reducing them. Thanks to the deployment of multiple independently targetable reentry vehicles (MIRV), both countries can now load their intercontinental ballistic missiles with more nuclear warheads than before.

It is 12 Minutes to Midnight, 1972: The United States and Soviet Union attempt to curb the race for nuclear superiority by signing the Strategic Arms Limitation Treaty (SALT) and the Anti-Ballistic Missile (ABM) Treaty. The two treaties force a nuclear parity of sorts. SALT limits the number of ballistic missile launchers either country can possess, and the ABM Treaty stops an arms race in defensive weaponry from developing.

It is 10 Minutes to Midnight: 1969: Nearly all of the world's nations come together to sign the Nuclear Non-Proliferation Treaty. The deal is simple—the nuclear weapon states vow to help the treaty's non-nuclear weapon signatories develop nuclear power if they promise to forego producing nuclear weapons. The nuclear weapon states also pledge to abolish their own arsenals when political conditions allow for it. Although Israel, India, and Pakistan refuse to sign the treaty, the *Bulletin* is cautiously optimistic: "The great powers have made the first step. They must proceed without delay to the next one—the dismantling, gradually, of their own oversized military establishments."

It is 7 Minutes to Midnight, 1968: Regional wars rage. U.S. involvement in Vietnam intensifies, India and Pakistan battle in 1965, and Israel and its Arab neighbors renew hostilities in 1967. Worse yet, France and China develop nuclear weapons to assert themselves as global players. "There is little reason to feel sanguine about the future of our society on the world scale," the *Bulletin* laments. "There is a mass revulsion against war, yes; but no sign of conscious intellectual leadership in a rebellion against the deadly heritage of international anarchy."

It is 12 Minutes to Midnight, 1963: After a decade of almost non-stop nuclear tests, the United States and Soviet Union sign the Partial Test Ban Treaty, which ends all atmospheric nuclear testing. While it does not outlaw underground testing, the treaty represents progress in at least slowing the arms race. It also signals awareness among the Soviets and United States that they need to work together to prevent nuclear annihilation.

It is 7 Minutes to Midnight, 1960: Political actions belie the tough talk of "massive retaliation." For the first time, the United States and Soviet Union appear eager to avoid direct confrontation in regional conflicts such as the 1956 Egyptian-Israeli dispute. Joint projects that build trust and constructive dialogue between third parties also quell diplomatic hostilities. Scientists initiate many of these measures, helping establish the International Geophysical Year, a series of coordinated, worldwide scientific observations, and the Pugwash Conferences, which allow Soviet and American scientists to interact.

Threat of Disaster in the 1950s and 1940s

It is 2 Minutes to Midnight, 1953: After much debate, the United States decides to pursue the hydrogen bomb, a weapon far more powerful than any atomic bomb. In October 1952, the United States tests its first thermonuclear device, obliterating a Pacific Ocean islet in the process; nine months later, the Soviets test an H-bomb of their own. "The hands of the Clock of Doom have moved again," the *Bulletin* announces. "Only a few more swings of the pendulum, and, from Moscow to Chicago, atomic explosions will strike midnight for Western civilization."

It is 3 Minutes to Midnight, 1949: The Soviet Union denies it, but in the fall, President Harry Truman tells the American public that the Soviets tested their first nuclear device, officially starting the arms race. "We do not advise Americans that doomsday is near and that they can expect atomic bombs to start falling on their heads a month or year from now," the *Bulletin* explains. "But we think they have reason to be deeply alarmed and to be prepared for grave decisions."

It is 7 Minutes to Midnight, 1947: As the *Bulletin* evolves from a newsletter into a magazine, the Clock appears on the cover for the first time. It symbolizes the urgency of the nuclear dangers that the magazine's founders—and the broader scientific community—are trying to convey to the public and political leaders around the world.

| *"If this sounds entirely subjective, that's because it is."*

The Doomsday Clock Does Not Provide a Good Gauge of World Danger

Michael Anton

Michael Anton is a senior editor in communications for the Ewing Marion Kauffman Foundation, and a former speechwriter for President George W. Bush. In the following viewpoint, he argues that the Doomsday Clock of the Bulletin of the Atomic Scientists *is partisan and inaccurate. He says that the clock is moved closer to midnight, signaling the approach of doomsday, whenever the United States fails to follow the* Bulletin's *liberal nuclear agenda. Anton concludes that the clock is a political stunt and has no relationship to the actual real world threat of nuclear destruction.*

As you read, consider the following questions:

1. How did the Doomsday Clock begin its life, according to Anton?

Michael Anton, "For Whom the Clock Ticks," *Weekly Standard*, January 14, 2010. Copyright © 2010 The Weekly Standard LLC—A Weekly Conservative Magazine & Blog. All rights reserved. Reproduced by permission.

2. What does Anton say is the gravest nuclear threat facing America today?

3. Anton says that President Barack Obama is more committed to arms control than any administration since which President?

Today [January 14, 2010] at 10:00 a.m., the so-called "doomsday clock"—a masterful PR [public relations] effort run by the anti-nuclear *Bulletin of Atomic Scientists*—will be reset for only the 19th time in its 62-year history.

The Clock Is Partisan

The clock is probably, after the national debt counter in Times Square, the most famous virtual government watchdog ever created. Except, unlike the former effort, it is necessarily—and maddeningly—imprecise. The only thing reliable about the clock is its partisanship.

The clock began life as cover art for an issue of the *Bulletin* in 1947, the dawn of the nuclear age. The hands were set to seven minutes to midnight as a sign that the end was nigh. It caused such a stir that the *Bulletin* was persuaded to make the clock its chief marketing tool and mascot. When the editors—made up almost wholly of left-leaning physicists and engineers who work in the nuclear field—feel that the world is hurtling faster toward nuclear disaster, they call a press conference, unveil a new graphic with the minute hand closer to midnight, and explain why. When they think things have moved in the right direction, the minute hand goes backward.

If this sounds entirely subjective, that's because it is. One of the things that made the Cold War so tense as the *Bulletin* would have to be the first to acknowledge, was the possibility that at any time, superpower conflict could have escalated—or stumbled—into a nuclear exchange with very little warning.

Indeed, nuclear disaster could well have struck on the day after a press conference in which the clock's minute hand was jubilantly moved backward.

Not Set to the Real World

That it never happened at all is another testament to the clock's inaptness to the real world of nuclear development, deployments, deterrence, and gamesmanship. The most amount of time the clock has ever allowed us was 17 minutes (after the signing of the [Strategic Arms Reduction Treaty] START I treaty in 1991). So shouldn't we have all been incinerated 17 minutes—or days, or weeks, or months, or years—ago?

Similarly, the gravest nuclear threat facing America today is the detonation of a terrorist-delivered nuclear device in the heart of one of our great cities. The clock has virtually nothing to say about that eventuality, which of course could happen at any moment—in five minutes or five years.

In truth, what the clock really gauges is *Bulletin* editors' approval or disapproval of the incumbent administration's commitment to the arms control agenda of the antiwar and anti-nuclear left. Causes for losing a minute almost always boil down to some significant victory for that agenda, and for gaining one, some defeat. Hence, when the United States withdrew from the Anti-Ballistic Missile Treaty in 2002 (in order to move ahead developing systems that might save American lives), the scientists subtracted two minutes. But when we initially signed the treaty in 1972, they added two.

The most recent change came in 2007, ostensibly as a response to North Korea's first nuclear test. But it was couched in anti-[George W.] Bush rhetoric that seemed incongruous given the Bush administration's second term turn toward accommodation, deal-making, and near-appeasement with North Korea.

So what's going to happen today? We won't know until ten o'clock. But the smart money is on the minute hand moving backward. [The hand was moved backward.] The [Barack] Obama administration has shown itself to be more committed to arms control than any since President [Jimmy] Carter's, and no administration has ever talked more about disarmament. Indeed, this President has called for a "nuclear free world"—and unlike President [Ronald] Reagan, who also wished for such a thing but was more hard-headed about the prospects for achieving it, Obama seems determined to start down the path no matter what other nuclear players do, and at significant cost to America's nuclear position.

Periodical and Internet Sources Bibliography

The following articles have been selected to supplement the diverse views presented in this chapter.

Cecil Adams	"Was All That Money Spent on Y2K Wasted?" *Straight Dope*, July 17, 2009. www.straightdope.com.
Benjamin Anastas	"The Final Days," *New York Times*, July 1, 2007. www.nytimes.com.
Scott Brown	"Scott Brown on Why the Doomsday Clock Needs to Be Abolished," *Wired*, October 2010. www.wired.com/magazine/.
Dennis Dutton	"It's Always the End of the World As We Know It," *New York Times*, December 31, 2009. www.nytimes.com.
George Lawton	"2010 Rings in Some Y2K-like Problems," *Computing Now*, January 2010. www.computer.org.
Tony Long	"Dec. 31, 1999: Horror or Hype? Y2K Arrives and the World Trembles," *Wired*, December 31, 2007. www.wired.com.
G. Jeffrey MacDonald	"Does Maya Calendar Predict 2012 Apocalypse?" *USA Today*, March 27, 2007. www.usatoday.com.
Ian O'Neill	"Doomsday Fabrication: Abusing Science and Making Money," Astroengine.com, August 21, 2008. www.astroengine.com.
Keith B. Payne	"Precision Prediction," *National Review Online*, January 18, 2010. www.nationalreview.com.
Dan Zak	"Doomsday Clock Set Back by a Minute," *Washington Post*, January 15, 2010.

OPPOSING
VIEWPOINTS®
SERIES

What Are Some Conflicts Involving Religious Doomsday Scenarios?

Chapter Preface

The Aum Shinrikyo was a violent, apocalyptic religious cult based in Japan. It was founded in 1987 by Shoko Asahara. Asahara based the religion on a combination of Buddhist and Christian beliefs, including the book of Revelation and the prophetic writings of 16th century astrologer Nostradamus. Aum Shinrikyo taught that there would be major disasters on earth before the year 2000, and also promised supernatural powers to its followers. The group eventually reached a membership of 20,000, many "attracted by the group's rejection of the corruption and materialism which they saw throughout modern Japan," according to B.A. Robinson in an August 19, 2006, article on ReligiousTolerance.org.

In preparation for the apocalypse, Aum Shinrikyo established chemical factories and stockpiled various dangerous chemicals. In the mid-1990s, the group launched a number of terrorist attacks within Japan. In March 1994, they released a cloud of deadly sarin nerve gas in a residential neighborhood which was home to judges sitting on a panel overseeing a real estate dispute involving the cult. The gas killed seven and hospitalized at least 200.

The most spectacular Aum Shinrikyo attack, however, occurred a year later on March 20, 1995. That morning, "packages were placed on five different trains in the Tokyo subway system. The packages consisted of plastic bags filled with a chemical mix and wrapped inside newspapers," according to Kyle B. Olson in a 1999 article in *Emerging Infectious Diseases*. The bags were punctured and the mix allowed to spill into the cars. The moving trains spread the deadly gas throughout Tokyo. All together, Olson continued, "The number injured in the attacks was just under 3,800. Of those, nearly 1,000 actually required hospitalization. . . . And 12 people were dead."

Following the attacks, Aum Shinrikyo members were prosecuted. Shoko Asahara, the cult's leader, was arrested and convicted; as of 2010 he was awaiting the death penalty. The group as a whole was not outlawed, but its membership shrank drastically. In 2007, the group split "due to internal friction over attempts to moderate the cults' religious beliefs and improve its public images," according to Holly Fletcher in a May 28, 2008, article on the Council of Foreign Relations website. The cult changed its name to "Aleph" in 2000. As of 2008, it has only about 1,650 members. It continues to be monitored by the Japanese police.

The following viewpoints look at other religious views of doomsday, and the effects of those beliefs.

"Cults provide a milieu where black-and-white thinking can grow and devour minds."

Psychological Factors Can Explain Apocalyptic Doomsday Cults

Peter A. Olsson

Peter A. Olsson is a psychiatrist, psychoanalyst, and author. In the following viewpoint, he argues that cult leaders and cult followers are bound together by psychological factors involving the failure to properly integrate narcissism, or self-love. Olsson also argues that cult leaders use psychological brain-washing techniques to bind cult members to them. He concludes that the power of cult leaders over their followers is dangerous and must be understood and stopped.

As you read, consider the following questions:

1. Olsson says that an appropriate amount of narcissism is necessary for what?

Peter A. Olsson, *Malignant Pied Pipers of Our Time: A Psychological Study of Destructive Cult Leaders from Rev. Jim Jones to Osama Bin Laden*, Keene, NH: PublishAmerica, 2005. Copyright © 2005 by Peter A. Olsson, M.D. Reproduced by permission of the author.

2. According to a study by W. Bion, small groups under stress and without clear, effective leadership will display what kinds of behavior?

3. In terrorist leader Osama bin Laden's al Qaeda camps, what does Olsson say recruits received besides military training?

To understand the powerful pull of a cult, we turn to the psychological concept of narcissism. The dynamics of narcissism are poignantly applicable to our study of powerful cult leaders as well as to the loyalty and devotion found in their followers.

Regardless of our relative strength or weakness, most of us search for meaningful affiliation and self-esteem to build significance or meaning in our lives. Most of us gradually gain enough independence, wisdom, and ability to think critically so that our self-love is solid; we do not allow other people, no matter how charismatic, to dominate our core values or decision-making process. Some less individuated people do not seem to be so resilient at some phases of their life, for various reasons of circumstance, disposition, or chance. The psychoanalytic term for this complex area of self-love and dignity is narcissism, or the narcissistic sector of our personality.

It is important to note that narcissism is *not* a psychoanalytic curse word and is not a synonym for selfishness or self-absorption. In a normal personality, self-love matures and develops in a healthy way, just as one's ability to love others expands and matures.

It was Sigmund Freud [founder of psychoanalysis] who first observed that we love *anaclitically* (relating to the mother who nurtured us or the father who protected us) or *narcissistically* (relating to the self we wish we were, the self we used to be, or in affiliation with another self that reflects favorably upon us). Anaclitic literally means "leaning on," and refers to an infant's utter dependence on its mother or mother substi-

Estimate of Death Toll from Cults

Jonestown (Jim Jones)	918
Tokyo (Asahara)	12
DiMambro/Jouret (Solar Temple)	69
Waco (Koresh)	90
Applewhite (Heavens Gate)	39
Manson & Family	40
Total	**1,168**

TAKEN FROM: Peter A. Olsson, *Malignant Pied Pipers of Our Time: A Psychological Study of Destructive Cult Leaders from Rev. Jim Jones to Osama Bin Laden*, Frederick, MD: PublishAmerica, 2005.

tute for its sense of well-being and actual survival. Anaclitic love is normal behavior in childhood, but not in adulthood.

Narcissistic love is neither "good" nor "bad" in itself; an appropriate amount of narcissism is necessary for healthy self-esteem, empathy, and creative expression. Too much or too little narcissism interferes with a person's relationships with others: a deficit of narcissistic love often causes low self-esteem and feelings of shame or rage; an excess is associated with arrogance, entitlement, and self-centeredness.

When we mature and individuate (i.e, develop our own individual personalities, separate and distinct from all others) with relative freedom, we integrate the love we have found in our parental figures and move along in our own struggles and mistakes in loving. . . . Cult leaders and followers get seriously stuck in these core issues. And in destructive apocalyptic cults, we . . . [see] how unloving the ultimate destiny of fanatical love can be.

The Cult Leader

The leader is crucial to any group. When a healthy group has an ethical, rational, and caring leader, it functions smoothly. A good or healthy spiritual leader helps facilitate rational decision-making within the group; exhibits incorruptible honesty; makes decisions with empathy and realism; shares leadership and cultivates it in younger members of the group; encourages individual freedom and dignity; respects members' families; and helps the group with positive projects that help the community at large. In times of great stress, healthy leadership matters even more. Think of New York City on 9/11 [2001] when leaders and people pulled together to help victims of the terrorist attacks.

In groups that lack an effective, healthy leader, external stress causes negative and regressive behavior. W. Bion, who studied group dynamics in the 1950s, offers valuable perspectives. He observed that in small groups (fewer than 15 members) under stress and without clear, effective leadership, members tend to fall into three main emotional patterns: dependency, fight-flight, and pairing. That is, they idealize the leader as omniscient and omnipotent and see themselves as immature and inadequate; they often are drawn to a paranoid leader who will lead the fight against external enemies; and they often focus on a couple who will (in the group's unconscious fantasy) survive the stress and ensure the longevity of the group. A cohesive group that feeds a leader's malignant narcissism and is fed hate in return only supersedes the self-absorbed, cruel, tyrannical, and sadistic qualities of the leader.

In larger groups (including whole communities and even societies) under stress and without a healthy leader, the relationship between leader and followers is not that of a benevolent shepherd and flock, but rather a reverberating, symbiotic "two-way street" in which members identify closely with each other, idealize the leader, and rally around him. In Waco [Texas] or Jonestown [Guyana], very few followers fled from [David] Koresh or [Jim] Jones.[1] For another example of this "circle-the-wagons" reaction, think back to 1997 in Iraq. When

1. David Koresh led the Branch Davidians, a sect in Waco, Texas, which was raided by the FBI in 1993, resulting in 75 deaths. Jim Jones led the Peoples Temple, a cult whose members all committed suicide on November 18, 1978.

the United States and its allies threatened action against [Iraqi president] Saddam Hussein, his followers formed a human shield around his palaces. . . .

The Dangerous Lure of Cults

Many clergy and even experienced mental health professionals underestimate the scope and power of cult leaders and their lieutenants in controlling the minds of their recruits. For example, David Koresh, . . . did not utilize some innocent ideological salesmanship, but rather a powerful, repetitive, mind-controlling indoctrination over days and weeks and months that wore down a victim's psychic reserves to the point of snapping or *thought reform*. In [terrorist leader Osama] bin Laden's Al Qaeda camps, in addition to military training, recruits received daily study of the Koran (something that attracted John Walker Lindh [an American who joined al Qaeda] and others) and radical Islamist theology and indoctrination. The recruits were discouraged from communicating with their families. Recruits treasured their meetings with bin Laden, and many of them were given new names by the terror organization.

In 1983, Dr. John G. Clark, Jr. grasped the significance of this issue. In a paper entitled "On the Further Study of Destructive Cultism," he wrote that too many clinicians "tend still to explain cult conversions, as well as the difficulties arising from them, as results of long-standing personality or familial problems, as expressions of normal developmental crises, or even as manifestations of formal mental disorders. These observers tend to ignore the necessary role played by the cult milieu in causing the radical personality changes and family schisms that have clearly affected so many previously normal people and well-integrated families."

In a 1987 paper, I added a corollary: "This blurring of clinical and phenomenological cause and effect has led to much confusion and dangerous casualness about destructive cults as if they were the benign, relatively harmless variety." Cults provide a milieu where black-and-white thinking can grow and devour minds.

> *"Among sociologists who study religion and social change, there is consensus that the term* cult *can be dangerous when it is applied as a pejorative label to all religious groups that are outside the mainstream of religious organizations."*

Sociological Factors Can Explain Apocalyptic Doomsday Cults

William Kornblum

William Kornblum is a professor of sociology at the City University of New York. In the following viewpoint, he argues that sects and cults are often formed by those outside social hierarchies in order to achieve more personal religious experience. He argues that prejudice against these cults can result in dangerous situations. He points to the encounters with the Branch Davidians in Waco, Texas, in 1993, and with Ghost Dance worshippers in Wounded Knee, South Dakota, in the 1890s. In both cases, Kornblum concludes, irrational fears of cult beliefs on the part of the government resulted in unnecessary violent action and the deaths of innocents.

William Kornblum, *Sociology in a Changing World, 8th ed.* Belmont, CA: Thomson Higher Education, 2008. Copyright © 2008 Thomson Learning, Inc. All rights reserved. Reproduced by permission.

As you read, consider the following questions:

1. According to the viewpoint, what do H. Richard Niebuhr and Max Weber agree is a primary cause of sect formation?

2. According to Nancy Ammerman, what is one of the primary interpretive lenses through which the general public views groups such as the Branch Davidians?

3. After a tragedy like Waco or Wounded Knee, who does Kornblum say the public blames for the deaths of cult members?

Sects and cults are a major source of change in religious organizations. People who are not satisfied with more established churches and denominations, or are otherwise alienated from society, often form or join a cult or sect. One of the most convincing explanations of the emergence of sects was suggested by H. Richard Niebuhr, borrowing from Max Weber's pioneering analysis of churches and sects. According to Weber, churches tend to justify the presence of inequality and stratification because they must appeal to people of all classes. Sects, on the other hand, may be led by charismatic individuals who appeal to people who have felt the sting of inequality. Niebuhr agreed with Weber that class conflict is a primary cause of sect formation. But he observed that as a sect becomes more successful and better organized, it becomes more like a church and begins to justify existing systems of stratification. This creates the conditions in which new sects may emerge.

Cults and Dissatisfaction

Another motivation for the formation of sects or cults is dissatisfaction with the interactions that occur in more established organizations. In church rituals, for example, prayer is often led by a priest or other religious professional and is relatively restrained, whereas in sects and cults communication between God and the individual is more direct and typically allows the individual to express deep emotions. The differing styles of interaction in different types of religious organizations can be illustrated by the contrast between the hierarchy of statuses and roles that characterizes the Catholic Church (with its pope, cardinals, bishops, priests, and other well-defined statuses) and the seemingly greater equality and looser structure of a cult like Krishna Consciousness or the Unification Church.

People who are attracted to cults are often influenced by a charismatic leader who inspires them to new and very personal achievements, such as ecstatic experiences, a sense of salvation, or a release from physical or psychological suffering. Some become cult members simply because they are lonely; others are born to cult members and are socialized into the cult.

Some, but by no means all, cults are extremely authoritarian and punitive. Their leaders may demand that members cut themselves off entirely from family and friends and sacrifice everything for the sake of the cult. The leaders may also insist that they themselves are above the moral teachings to which their followers must adhere. Under these conditions of isolation and submission to a dominant authority, cult members may be driven to incredible extremes of behavior—even mass suicide, as occurred in the case of the followers of Heaven's Gate in 1997. However, not all cults are so dangerous or so easily condemned, and there is an ongoing conflict between norms that protect the right of individuals to belong to cults and efforts to protect people from the harm that can occur when cult leaders place themselves above morality and the law.

Waco and Wounded Knee

The confrontation that took place in Waco, Texas, on February 28, 1993, between the Branch Davidians and agents of the

Bureau of Alcohol, Tobacco, and Firearms (BATF) revealed the need for greater understanding of alternative religious groups. Among sociologists who study religion and social change, there is consensus that the term *cult* can be dangerous when it is applied as a pejorative label to all religious groups that are outside the mainstream of religious organizations.

Nancy Ammerman, one of the foremost authorities on Protestant religious groups in the United States, notes that "one of the primary interpretive lenses through which the general public views groups such as the Branch Davidians is the lens supplied by 'cult awareness' groups and 'exit counselors.' Namely, most people think members of a group like the Branch Davidians must have been 'brainwashed' into joining". Analyses of the Waco tragedy now place greater emphasis on the deep misunderstandings that existed between the government agencies, primarily the FBI [Federal Bureau of Investigation] and the BATF, that laid siege to the Branch Davidian community, and the members of the community—especially its leader, David Koresh. These misunderstandings appear to have been deepened by hysterical press and television coverage during the episodes of violence and siege.

Sociologist Joel Martin observes that the Branch Davidians were not newcomers but an established alternative religious group that had lived in the Waco area since the mid-1930s. The group did believe in an unconventional variant of Seventh-Day Adventist millenarianism and that Armageddon and the end of time were close at hand. They also had some unorthodox and disturbing sexual practices, but these charges, and the charge that they were stockpiling weapons, could have been addressed by quietly apprehending the group's leader for questioning rather than engaging in the large-scale operation that resulted in an armed standoff and the eventual death of the entire group in a blaze of fire and bullets.

Many sociologists point to the similarities between the Waco disaster and the tragedy at Wounded Knee, South Dakota, in 1890. In both cases (and many others like them), a new religion attracts men and women with visions of a new heaven and earth. As they seek to live in accord with these visions, they withdraw into their own community, altering their behavior in ways that may seem strange and even threatening to others. People outside the community begin to spread rumors about them. Government authorities get nervous and plan to move against the group. Journalists congregate, anticipating a big story. When a confrontation takes place, gunfire erupts and a few of the authorities are killed. In the end, the millenarian [that is apocalyptic] community is destroyed. After the tragedy, officials, scholars, historians, and journalists interpret what happened. Many conclude that the community's members had been caught up in a "messiah craze." Thus the dead are blamed for their own deaths.

Such was the case with the Lakota Indian Ghost Dancers who were killed at Wounded Knee in 1890. In the Ghost Dance religion, some Indians began to believe they might be invulnerable to white attackers. In a sense, they courted death at the hands of white men. Many believed that if the Ghost Dance did not protect them, they would at least achieve speedy transport to a happier existence than the one they led among the conquering white people. The situation of the Branch Davidians killed outside Waco a century later was similar. The issue is not whether either group was right or wrong but how people in a position to bring understanding to these tragic situations can help prevent similar events from occurring over and over again.

"Dispensationalists want to bring about world events that would have catastrophic implications for other Christians and for non-Christians."

Belief in the Rapture Is Theologically and Politically Dangerous

Bill Barnwell

Bill Barnwell is a pastor and has written for The American Conservative, *LewRockwell.com, and Antiwar.com, among other publications. In the following viewpoint, he argues against dispensationalism, a popular apocalyptic Christian worldview. Dispensationalism, Barnwell says, believes in an interpretation of the Bible which holds that the world will get worse and war is inevitable. Thus, Barnwell says, most dispensationalists are militarists who argue that trying to improve the world is wrong. Barnwell concludes that this position is un-Biblical. It is also dangerous, since some dispensationalists are in position to influence US political decisions.*

Bill Barnwell, "The Troubling Worldview of the 'Raptue-Ready' Christian," LewRock well.com, February 2, 2007. Copyright © 2007 LewRockwell.com. Reproduced by permission of the publisher and author.

As you read, consider the following questions:

1. Who is John Hagee, and what does Barnwell say he believes is prophetically inevitable?

2. According to Barnwell, dispensationalists believe that the only two options for human action are to hand the world over to Satan or to believe what?

3. Dispensationalists believe war is kind of good and peace is kind of bad based on what reasoning, according to Barnwell?

When the subject of the "end-times" comes up, many Christians and non-Christians don't want to talk about it. Some Christians, annoyed with all the competing theories and terminology just say, "What difference does it make? Jesus is coming back and I just need to be ready." Non-Christians just assume that since Christianity isn't true, then the whole issue doesn't matter. Well, actually, it does matter. I will submit that the popular doctrines of the *Left Behind* series [a popular series of Christian novels dealing with the end times] pose very real threats not only to Christianity, but also to the wider culture.

The Final Generation

Probably most conservative Protestants (though not all of us) believe that humanity is certainly in the final generation of life on earth as we currently know it. Not that we "could be," but that "we must be." That's a big distinction. They believe this because of their views on a couple key Biblical texts. The first is the Olivet Discourse. This discourse by Jesus about the "end of the age" can be found in Mark 13, Matthew 24, and Luke 21. Dispensationalists—a group that believes God has two separate prophetic programs for Israel and the Church and generally believes that Christians will be removed from the earth before a final tribulation—see all of the events or signs spoken of by Jesus as referring to events that are happening now or going to happen very soon. Never mind that Jesus was first and foremost referring to events that would occur within his own disciples' lifetime (Matthew 24:34). They believe that nothing past chapter 3 in the book of Revelation has occurred yet. It is all in the future, and all relates to the tribulation period, which true Christians will avoid.

Another key text is Daniel 9:27. It is from this verse alone that we get the idea of a "seven-year tribulation" during the end times. But the New Testament says nothing about a seven-year tribulation. The book of Revelation refers to a 3.5-year period—five different times. They are most likely referring to the same time period. Dispensationalists believe by prophetic necessity a number of things. First, they assume that the world must get worse in just about all ways. Second, they assume that Daniel 9:27 calls for the rebuilding of a Third Jewish Temple at the site of the Dome of the Rock. Therefore, prophetic necessity demands that the current Islamic al-Aqsa mosque must be torn down to build this new Jewish Temple. Halfway through the tribulation period, the antichrist will come and exalt himself in the new Jewish Temple, stop sacrifices in the Temple, break a peace treaty he had earlier made with Israel, and proclaim himself to be God. They get all this from cutting and pasting Daniel 9:27, Matthew 24:15, 2 Thessalonians 2:4 together and then associating those passages with everything that will be going on in Revelation 4–19.

There are all sorts of problems with these interpretations. First of all, the New Testament says nothing about a "pretribulational rapture."[1] . . .

Dangerous Doctrine

Once you begin thinking of the implications involved, you begin to see why this doctrine is so dangerous to everybody.

---

1. The rapture is a moment when the godly are taken up into heaven. The "pretribulational rapture" means the rapture will occur before the end times, which the non-raptured will have to suffer through.

'Then again it could just be a break in the clouds!'

"Then again it could be a break in the clouds!" by Mike Mosedale. www.Cartoon Stock.com.

Dispensationalists seem to have a preoccupation with war. In fact, right now, dispensationalist mega-church pastor John Hagee is preaching that a war with Iran is not only the right thing to do, but is prophetically inevitable. Apparently, Bible prophecy demands a showdown with Iran. You see, if you aren't on the side of war, then you aren't on the side of God. Talk of peace now becomes irrelevant. It's *God's will* that we be militarists. In fairness, not all dispensationalists are militarists. . . . But they are in a definite minority. The prevailing worldview of dispensationalism glorifies war, militarism, and the State.

The dispensationalist view of Daniel 9:27 provides some troubling implications as well. They don't care that tearing down the al-Aqsa mosque would result in a regional war and cause all sorts of global distress. This would not be a bad thing in their minds. They believe that it was all foreordained and is a sign that the end of the world would be soon upon us.

Also, if you buy into these interpretations, talks of peace in the Middle East are futile. Jews and Muslims must continue killing each other at high rates. And who will be the one bringing peace to the Middle East in this popular end-time paradigm? Not Jesus, but the Antichrist. Therefore, talk of Middle East peace during this current "dispensation" is not from Jesus, but the Antichrist. When dispensationalists hear talk of peace summits or treaties in the Middle East, they assume it must have evil origins and be antichristic. If that's the cause, why bother trying to make the world a better place? All we need to do is be good Christians and wait for our ticket out of this earth and make way for the Antichrist.

Dispensationalists are numerous and popular. Well-connected preachers like Hagee have political connections. Dispensational preachers and lobbyists have the ear of the White House and are directly trying to influence foreign policy based on their very questionable theological views, which, by the way, are less than 200 years old. This is more than just a quirky theology that doesn't affect those who do not hold it. Dispensationalists want to bring about world events that would have catastrophic implications for other Christians and for non-Christians.

Against Change for the Better

If they are correct, why should any of us bother trying to make the world a better place? Dispensationalists get very annoyed at this question. They say, "Final peace on earth will only come through Christ!" They basically insist Christians trying to do good in the world should only focus on "spiritual things." Trying to change social institutions for the better is futile and presumptuous. Apparently the only two options are handing the world over to Satan or believing that humans can do everything in their own strength. Not much room for nuance here.

Ironically, many dispensationalists are involved in the Religious Right movement and want to stem abortions, ban gay marriage and make America more Christian. But at the same time they believe in a theology that says the world can only get worse, that there's nothing any of us can do about it, and that it's about to get so bad Christians are going to be taken off of the earth. If the ship is irreversibly sinking, why try and patch up the leaks?

If you need more proof that many dispensationalists hold troubling worldviews, just take a visit over to the Rapture Ready message board. The main site is one of the bigger dispensationalist/pretribulational sites on the web. You can read for yourselves how they view the world, how they can't wait to escape it, and their obsession with war.

One angry pre-tribber wrote me a few weeks back. He had this to say:

> When the RAPTURE of the CHURCH takes place, and mark my words it will, maybe them you will see the light! After you have been left behind you are going to look back on all the people that you deceived, who will probably be in your face at that time, and hopefully repent of the false gospel that you were teaching! It's not to late to be saved during the 7 year tribulation period but it will be harder when you hear that Christians, who become Christians after the Rapture of the Church, are being beheaded for the witness of Jesus! Hopefully you and those who partake of your beliefs will see the light before Christ comes for the Church!

War Is Good, Peace Is Bad

Notice in his mind I'm not even a real Christian. The reason? Because I happen to have a different position than he does on the issue of the "rapture." I'll also apparently be too much of a coward to "convert" during the "7 year tribulation" because other people who become Christians after the pre-tribulational rapture are being beheaded. Ever notice with people who so strongly believe this doctrine that they assume everyone who will be "left behind" is going to be absolutely clueless? Maybe I too will just assume aliens came and abducted the "true Christians." Apparently I'd be too scared to be beheaded, even though I'd find myself instantly in heaven along with all the real Christians who were taken up in the rapture.

Finally, notice the great confidence of this guy. He is so convinced of his position that only an idiot or heretic would disagree. Well, I challenge people like this, and the crew over at Rapture Ready to actually put their interpretations up against the Scriptures and think about the logic and implications of their beliefs.

The logic and implications are clear. Society is going to hades in a handbasket. There's little we can do to stem the tide of evil. The Middle East must further deteriorate. Anyone who disagrees with Israel's foreign policy is opposing God. The third most important site to Muslims must be crushed to make way for a new Jewish Temple. Good Christians should support the building of a new temple with new animal sacrifices taking place inside of it. . . . And in a strange sense, war is kinda good and peace is kinda bad—since war is a sign that the end is near and peace on earth is a sign of the Antichrist. Any Christian who doesn't agree with all this is deceived at best and a heretic at worst.

When you understand that millions of Christians believe this way, and that some of them are actually fairly influential on the political scene, you begin to see why this theology needs to be refuted. By refuting it, dispensationalists think you're trying to refute God. I would argue that you're being more faithful to God and the very Scriptures themselves. This is not just an in-house debate that only affects myself and other Christians. Dispensationalists have a vision for the world and it is bad news for everybody. Therefore, it would do you all good to spend some time in the Bible and see what exactly the Scriptures have to say on this subject.

> *"The Rapture is not provided so Christians can sit smugly on the sidelines with a smiley face and wave bye-bye to a Hell bound world. It is the hope of deliverance from the Wrath of God held by those who . . . proclaim the Word of God at the risk of alienation, persecution, torture and death."*

If Understood Correctly, Belief in the Rapture Is Not Dangerous

Paul Proctor

Paul Proctor is a writer and columnist. In the following viewpoint, he argues that the Rapture is no excuse not to resist evil in the world. However, he argues that the Rapture, when believing Christians are taken up into Heaven leaving non-believers behind, is promised in Scripture. He says that those who try to make the world a perfect place are deceived, because the world is destined to be destroyed by God. But, he says, Christians must confront the world and proclaim the Word of God in the face of persecution in order to be worthy of the Rapture.

Paul Proctor, "The Rapture Is Coming—Believe It Or Not," NewsWithViews.com, February 8, 2006. Reproduced by permission of NewsWithViews.com. http://www.newswith views.com/PaulProctor/proctor87.htm.

As you read, consider the following questions:

1. According to Proctor, how do many postmodern Christians interpret the injunction to turn the other cheek?

2. What does Proctor say Christians should do rather than cite the latest poll or embrace the latest church teaching?

3. Proctor argues that those who attempt to build God's Kingdom on Earth will end up serving whom?

There is an enormous controversy brewing among professing Christians today as to whether or not there is going to be a Rapture[1] of the Church. Many who criticize those who believe in the Rapture do so, not out of an understanding of scripture but rather out of a zealous resentment for lazy, complacent and irresponsible Christians shirking their duty to resist evil in the world.

Christians Must Confront Evil

I couldn't agree more that there is a systemic failure on the part of the church today to confront evil and rebuke sin. It is a theme that has become a trademark of this column. Satan has clearly made capitulating cronies out of many postmodern Christians, convincing them that *"turning the other cheek"* actually means looking the other way, when it comes to addressing overt transgressions against God and man, leading the Church at large into an immoral pact of sorts that says: *For the sake of Results and Relationships, I won't criticize your sin if you won't criticize mine.*

But friends, this is nothing short of organized crime against The Almighty for the gratification, glorification, and justification of sinful man. It encourages us to convert God's grace into spiritual spinelessness so we can have our cake and eat it too and be called a Witness for Jesus Christ without ac-

1. The Rapture is a predicted moment when believing Christians will be taken into Heaven by God, leaving non-believers behind.

tually having to act like one or suffer any personal loss or adverse consequences for our professed faith in the only begotten Son of God.

Scripture, in fact, teaches something totally different:

> "Them that sin rebuke before all, that others also may fear."—1st Timothy 5:20

> "And have no fellowship with the unfruitful works of darkness, but rather reprove them."—Ephesians 5:11

These scriptures illustrate with crystal clarity the illegitimacy of the church growth movement and its new reformation of sin-tolerant love; a seeker sensitivity that seduces Churchaterians into an effeminate faith that hides behind a positive-only, chit chat, save-my-self-esteem spirituality so as to protect and promote those sacred Results and Relationships that grow apostate fellowships into mega-mausoleums for the living dead by cordially inviting visitors and prospects to "connect" or "plug in" rather than "*repent*," and "*take up thy cross*" to follow Jesus as He commands.

Persecution vs. Wrath

However, do not let those who have rightly condemned the reckless neglect of cowardly Christians convince you that there will be no Rapture of the Church. It is not a handy escape from persecution, but rather a glorious deliverance from God's Wrath. Persecution and Wrath are two entirely different things; so don't make the mistake of confusing the two even though they may seem similar. That's where much of the confusion lies.

> "For God hath not appointed us to wrath, but to obtain salvation by our Lord Jesus Christ, Who died for us, that, whether we wake or sleep, we should live together with him."—1st Thessalonians 5:9–10

It is said: "If you want to know what God will do in the future, just look at what He has done in the past." That is why

Opinions of Christians about the Second Coming of Jesus Christ

| | Believe in 2nd Coming % | Time of Christ's return... | |
		Is Revealed in Bible %	In Your Lifetime %
Total	79	33	20
Total Protestant	83	36	23
Total Catholic	70	27	12
Bible is...			
Literal word of God	95	52	37
Word of God, not literal	76	24	11

TAKEN FROM: "Many Americans Uneasy with Mix of Religion and Politics," The Pew Forum on Religion and Public Life, August 24, 2006.

it is so crucial that we study the scriptures for answers to the issues of life rather than cite the latest poll or embrace the latest church teaching. God's Work and Will among men are recorded there for our instruction. But one has to believe God and search the scriptures faithfully to know what that instruction is; otherwise they will likely be led astray by the fashionable theories and passions of renown men and find themselves ensnared by Machiavellian machinations that come from the heart of rebellion.

Noah endured the wicked world around him; yet when it came time for God's Wrath to be poured out upon the Earth in the form of a great flood, he and his family were delivered from it in an Ark that the Lord commanded him to build. This is a type and shadow of the Rapture—an illustration for our edification of God protecting and rescuing His Own from judgment.

"But as the days of Noe were, so shall also the coming of the Son of man be. For as in the days that were before the flood they were eating and drinking, marrying and giving in marriage, until the day that Noe entered into the ark, And knew not until the flood came, and took them all away; so shall also the coming of the Son of man be. Then shall two be in the field; the one shall be taken, and the other left. Two women shall be grinding at the mill; the one shall be taken, and the other left. Watch therefore: for ye know not what hour your Lord doth come."—Matthew 24:37–42

A tormented Lot was patiently escorted out of Sodom and Gomorrah along with his family shortly before God's Wrath rained down fire and brimstone from the heavens. He too suffered for his faith in a wicked place; but in the end was Raptured away to safety in a Divine deliverance from God's Wrath.

"Likewise also as it was in the days of Lot; they did eat, they drank, they bought, they sold, they planted, they builded; But the same day that Lot went out of Sodom it rained fire and brimstone from heaven, and destroyed them all."—Luke 17:28–29

The Lord didn't command Moses to return to Egypt to conquer it, "transition it" or "transform it" into a godly place. Nor was he instructed to find common ground with Pharaoh, strike a deal, make friends or even learn how to get along with him for the sake of Results and Relationship. No, he was sent back to lead God's Chosen out of that wicked place because it was His Will that they be delivered; and it is still His Will today.

So as it was, so shall it be; the Rapture of God's Own; not from the growing persecution and hardship around us; but from the terrible Wrath that is coming upon the Earth as described in Revelation.

The Rapture Fits No Global Agenda

Those who endeavor to "change the world" and make it a better place for Christ and His Church or take it back by force or persuasion to build God's Kingdom here on Earth, by and large, reject or downplay the notion of a coming Rapture because it doesn't fit their global agenda or Dominionist worldview. Thinking they do God service, they in fact condemn those who look toward that glorious day of deliverance, not realizing, in their pride and delusion that the kingdom they build will soon be ruled by the antichrist, where many who call themselves Christians will worship and serve him thinking he is the Christ. Because they did not know or believe the Word of God but instead allowed themselves to be guided by their own pride, wisdom, emotions, ambitions and senses, they will be left to receive the "wages of sin."

> "And for this cause God shall send them strong delusion, that they should believe a lie: That they all might be damned who believed not the truth, but had pleasure in unrighteousness."—2nd Thessalonians 2:11–12

But still our Savior returns; and in the Father's time, to deliver those of us who are not ashamed at His coming!

> "For the Lord himself shall descend from heaven with a shout, with the voice of the archangel, and with the trump of God: and the dead in Christ shall rise first: Then we which are alive and remain shall be caught up together with them in the clouds, to meet the Lord in the air: and so shall we ever be with the Lord."—1st Thessalonians 4:16–17

The Rapture is not provided so Christians can sit smugly on the sidelines with a smiley face and wave bye-bye to a Hell bound world. It is the hope of deliverance from the Wrath of God held by those who courageously stand, speak out and proclaim the Word of God at the risk of alienation, persecution, torture and death that they may be counted worthy witnesses for Jesus Christ.

*"How about a revival of Christendom
as a concept—as a political concept?"*

Christian Solidarity Is Needed to Prevent Islam from Destroying the West

James P. Pinkerton

James P. Pinkerton is a writer and a fellow at the New America Foundation. He served in the administrations of Presidents Ronald Reagan and George H.W. Bush. In the following viewpoint, he argues that militant Islam is seriously threatening to overrun Europe. He argues that the West should revive a militant Christian identity to confront this threat. The West, including Europe, America, Latin America, and the Christian parts of Africa, should defend Israel and defend themselves, but should not invade Muslim territory. Pinkerton argues that such a vigilant separation would preserve Europe and peace.

As you read, consider the following questions:

1. Between 2004 and 2050, how much will the population of the Arab world increase, according to Pinkerton?

2. How does Pinkerton define "the Shire strategy"?

James P. Pinkerton, "The Once & Future Christendom," *American Conservative*, September 10, 2007. Reproduced by permission.

3. What strategy does Pinkerton suggest to reduce conflict in Africa?

In one of the great epics of Western literature, the hero, confronted by numerous and powerful enemies, temporarily gives in to weakness and self-pity. "I wish," he sighs, "none of this had happened." The hero's wise adviser responds, "So do all who live to see such times, but that is not for them to decide." The old man continues, "There are other forces at work in this world . . . besides the will of evil." Some events, he adds, are "meant" to be "And that is an encouraging thought."

Clash of Civilizations

Indeed it is. Perhaps, today, we are meant to live in these times. Perhaps right here, right now, we are meant to be tested. Maybe we are meant to have faith that other forces are at work in this world, that we are meant to rediscover our strength and our survival skills.

And so the question: can we, the people of the West, be brought to failure despite our enormous cultural and spiritual legacy? Three thousand years of history look down upon us: does this generation wish to be remembered for not having had the strength to look danger squarely in the eye? For having failed to harness our latent strength in our own defense?

With apologies to the frankenfood-fearers and polar bear-sentimentalizers, the biggest danger we face is the Clash of Civilizations, especially as we rub against the "bloody borders" of Islam.

What if, in the coming century, we lose that clash—and the source of our civilization? What if Muslims take over Europe? What if "Eurabia" indeed comes to pass? Would Islamic invaders demolish the Vatican, as the Taliban [radical religious Muslims who gained control of Afghanistan in the late 1990s] dynamited Afghanistan's Buddhas of Bamyan in 2001? Or would they settle merely for stripping the great cathedrals of

Europe of all their Christian adornment, rendering them into mosques? And what if the surviving non-Muslim population of Europe is reduced to subservient "dhimmitude" [non-Muslim minorities]?

It could happen. Many think it will. In July 2004 Princeton historian Bernard Lewis told Germany's *Die Welt* that Europe would be Islamic by the end of this century, "at the very latest." . . .

On the other side of the great divide, militant Muslims are feeling the wind at their backs. Last November [2006], Abu Ayyub al-Masri, leader of [terrorist organization] al-Qaeda in Mesopotamia, released an audiotape in which he vowed, "We will not rest from our *jihad* [holy war] until we are under the olive trees of the Roman Empire"—which is to say, much of Europe. This August [2007], Iranian president Mahmoud Ahmadinejad, traveling to Afghanistan, declared, "There is no way for salvation of mankind but rule of Islam over mankind." To be sure, there's no shortage of Christians who speak this way, but none of them are currently heads of state.

If demography is the author of destiny, then the danger of Europe falling within *dar al-Islam* is real. And in addition to the teeming Muslim lumpen already within the gates, plenty more are coming. According to United Nations data, the population of the Arab world will increase from 321 million in 2004 to 598 million in 2050. Are those swarming masses really going to hang back in Egypt and Yemen when Europe beckons? And of course, over the horizon, just past Araby, abide the Muslim multitudes of Central Asia and Africa, where tens of millions more would love to make the secular hajj [pilgrimage] to, say, Rome [Italy] or Berlin [Germany].

In other words, if present trends continue the green flag of Islam—bearing the *shahada*, the declaration of faith, "There is no god but God; Muhammad is the Messenger of God"—could be fluttering above Athens [Greece] and Rotterdam [Netherlands] in the lifespan of a youngster today. If so, then the glory of Europe as the hub of Greco-Roman and Christian civilization would be extinguished forever.

The Shire Strategy

If this Muslimization befalls Europe, the consequences would be catastrophic for Americans as well. Although some neoconservatives, bitter at Old European "surrender monkeys," might be quietly pleased at the prospect, the fact is that a Salafist Surge into the heart of Europe—destroying the civilization that bequeathed to us Aesop and Aristotle, Voltaire and the Victorians—would be a psychic wound that would never heal, not across the great sward of America, not even in the carpeted think-warrens of the American Enterprise Institute [a conservative think tank]. A dolorous bell would toll for all of us, scattered as we might be in the European Diaspora.

So for better ideas, we might turn to J.R.R. Tolkien. The medievalist-turned-novelist, best-known for *The Hobbit* and *The Lord of the Rings*, has been admired by readers and moviegoers alike for his fantastic flights. Yet we might make special note of his underlying political, even strategic, perspective. Amid all his swords and sorcery, we perhaps have neglected Tolkien's ultimate point: some things are worth fighting for—and other things are not worth fighting for; indeed, it is a tragic mistake even to try.

In his subtle way, Tolkien argues for a vision of individual and collective self-preservation that embraces a realistic view of human nature, including its limitations, even as it accepts difference and diversity. Moreover, Tolkien counsels robust self-defense in one's own area—the homeland, which he calls the Shire—even as he advocates an overall modesty of heroic ambition. All in all, that's not a bad approach for true conservatives, who appreciate the value of lumpy hodgepodge as opposed to artificially imposed universalisms.

So with Tolkien in mind, we might speak of the "Shire Strategy." It's simple: the Shire is ours, we want to keep it, and so we must defend it. Yet by the same principle, since others have their homelands and their rights, we should leave them alone, as long as they leave us alone. Live and let live. That's not world-historical, merely practical. For us, after our recent spasm of universalism—the dogmatically narcissistic view that everyone, everywhere wrests to be like us—it's time for a healthy respite, moving toward an each-to-his-own particularism. . . .

The Revival of Christendom

Two years ago [2005], the Eurocrats in Brussels [Belgium] drafted a 300-page EU [European Union] constitution that consciously omitted reference to Europe's specifically Christian heritage. The voters of France, as well as Holland, rejected that secular document.

Maybe there's a lesson here. The people of Europe might not be so eager, after all, to declare that they are "united in diversity." What does that phrase mean, anyway? How about trying to find something that unites Europeans in unity? How about a revival of Christendom as a concept—as a political concept? A revival, or at least a remembrance, of Europe's cultural heritage could be the healing force that Europe needs.

After all, it worked in the past. In the words of the 19th-century French historian Numa Denis Fustel de Coulanges, the victory of Christianity marked "the end of ancient society"—and all the petty divisions that went with it. Fustel de Coulanges continues, "Man felt that he had other obligations besides that of living and dying for the city. Christianity distinguished the private from the public virtues. By giving less honor to the latter, it elevated the former; it placed God, the family, the human individual above country, the neighbor above the city."

As history proves, a larger communion can be built on such sentiments. In the 9th century, Alcuin of York declared that the crowning of Charlemagne as the first Holy Roman

Emperor would bring forth a new *Imperium Christianum*. Ten centuries later, [historian] Hilaire Belloc asserted, "The Faith is Europe. And Europe is the Faith." Indeed, during those many centuries, Europe enjoyed a pretty good run. Only in the last century—the century of atheists, psychiatrists, and National Socialists—has Europe's survivability come into question. Today, the Christian author Os Guiness puts the issue plainly: "A Europe cut off from its spiritual roots cannot survive."

Some will smile at the thought that Christianity might be part of the solution to the problems of the Third Millennium. Admittedly, there's an element of faith in the idea of trying to revive the idea of Christian unity. But Christendom is the Shire Strategy, applied.

To keep the peace, we must separate our civilizations. We must start with a political principle, that the West shall stay the West, while the East can do as it wishes on its side of the frontier, and only on its side. The classical political maxim *cuius regio, eius religio* ("whose region, his religion") makes sense. To be sure, it has been unfashionable to talk this way in the West, but Muslims are avidly applying it as they set about martyring the remaining Christian populations of Iraq, Lebanon, and Egypt. So we of the West can build walls, as needed, and as physically imposing as need be. Going further, we can finally recognize the need for an energy-independence embargo, so that we no longer finance those who wish to conquer or kill us.

For obvious reasons, strategic as well as moral, the Western political alliance must be bigger than just a few relatively friendly countries along the other side of the Atlantic. It should include, most pressingly, Russia. Vladimir Putin [prime minister of Russia] might think of himself as a rival, even a foe, of the United States, but he knows he faces a mortal enemy in Islam; it's the Chechens who are killing his soldiers. So as Russia enjoys its own Christian revival, a reconciliation with mostly Christian America is possible. Immediately, America should renew the spirit of Ronald Reagan's 1983 Strategic Defense Initiative speech, in which the Gipper [Reagan] called for including Moscow [Russia] inside the protective shield. So instead of building missile-defense sites in Eastern Europe, dividing Europe from Russia, the United States should put those sites in Russia's southern reaches, to face the real enemy, which is Iran and the rest of nuclear Islam. Even Putin has suggested this defensive placement, perhaps because down deep, he, too, understands that the Christian West should be unified, not divided.

A Council of the West

But what of Christians elsewhere in the world? What, for example, of Latin America—which includes the likes of Fidel Castro [Cuban dictator] and Hugo Chavez [Venezuelan dictator]? And even more urgently, what of Africa, where Christians are suffering from many afflictions, including the inexorable Muslim advance, pushing south past the 10th parallel into the Christian populations of countries including Nigeria, Sudan, and Ethiopia? How to withstand these many challenges?

The answer: through political co-operation. In Tolkien's world, it was the Council of Elrond. Perhaps in our world, it could be Council of the West.

It's been done before. In AD 325, Constantine the Great convened the Council of Nicaea, drawing together quarrelsome bishops from across Europe to hammer out the basic doctrines of the church. Constantine was the first Christian Roman Emperor, although he concerned himself more with geopolitics than theological minutiae. "It is my desire," he told this first ecumenical convocation, "that you should meet together in a general council . . . and to know you are resolved to be in common harmony together." The council was a success, producing the Nicene Creed, which united European faith for centuries to come.

But today, how to find a new unity that reaches across oceans and continents, to include the likes of Putin and Chavez? Answer: with great difficulty, not all at once, and with no certainty of success.

And what of other hard cases? What of Africa? The Christian countries of Africa are part of the Shire Strategy and need to be embraced with tough love. The immediate mission is to delineate a Christian Zone and a Muslim Zone, dividing countries if need be. All Christians, and all Muslims, have a stake in minimizing conflict; the obvious way is by separating the combatants. So a wall should go up between the warring faiths, and then a bigger wall, until the flashpoint risk of civilization clash goes away. Then, and only then, might we hope to find workable solutions within the Christian Zone.

Some will insist that this neo-Constantinian vision of muscular political Christendom is implausible—or inimical to world peace. But in fact whether we like it or not, the world is forming into blocs. Samuel Huntington [a political scientist] was right about "the clash of civilizations"—but with political skill, we can keep clashes from becoming larger wars.

No matter what we say or do, the blocs of Hindus, Chinese, and Japanese are all going their separate cultural ways, rediscovering their own unique heritages. And Islam, of course, is at odds with all of its neighbors. In his book a decade ago, Huntington, mindful of the indirect danger posed by American universalism, was even more mindful of the direct danger posed by Muslims: "Islam's borders are bloody and so are its innards," he writes. "Muslim bellicosity and violence are late-twentieth century facts which neither Muslims nor non-Muslims can deny." That's bad news, but there's a silver lining: if Westerners, Russians, Africans, Hindus, and Chinese all feel threatened by Islam—and they all do—there's plenty of opportunity for a larger encircling alliance, with an eye toward feasible strategies of containment, even quarantine. But not conquest, not occupation, not "liberation." So the big question is whether or not Christians will continue to be divided into four blocs, as they are at present: Western, Russian, African, Latin. Can four smaller Christian blocs really become one big bloc? One Christendom? Perhaps—borrowing once again from Tolkien—such unification was meant to happen.

That is an encouraging thought: a Council of the West, bringing all the historically Christian countries of the world into one communion.

The Rescue of Israel

But what of Israel? If East is East and West is West, what of the Jewish state, which sits in the East? After all, the entire Middle Eastern region is looking more and more Mordor-like. Tolkien described that terrible wasteland: "High mounds of crashed and powdered rock, great cones of earth fire-blasted and poison-stained, stood like an obscene graveyard in endless rows, slowly revealed in the reluctant light." Not much hope there, at least for Westerners. Whatever possessed us to think we could make Muslims into our own image? . . .

We can make two points: first, Israel must survive, and second, on its current course, Israel will likely not survive.

In recent years, Israel finds its strategic situation worsening. It is increasingly confronted, not by incompetent tinhorn dictators but by determined Muslim jihadists, many of whom live in the Palestinian territories, some of whom live within Israel itself. Meanwhile, Iran proceeds with its nuclear program, while Pakistan, just a heartbeat away from Taliban-ification, already has its nukes in place, ready for export should the right *fatwa* [Islamic religious command] be uttered. And the Russians and the Chinese, empowered and lured by high energy prices, have their own designs on the region, which include no good tidings for Jews.

Unfortunately, if we look forthrightly into the future, we can see blood and fire ahead for Israel. Aside from the civilization-jolting moral tragedy of a Second Holocaust—a phrase used freely, albeit not lightly, by such Jewish observers as Philip Roth and Ron Rosenbaum—there would be the physical devastation of the Holy Land. How would Christians recover from the demolition of the Church of the Holy Sepulcher in Jerusalem? How would Diasporic Jews absorb the Temple Mount's obliteration? And how, for that matter, would Muslims react to the detonation of the Noble Sanctuary, which sits atop that mount?

Any destruction of Israel would be accompanied, one way or another, by the destruction of much of the Middle East. . . .

Some say that the solution to Middle Eastern problems is some sort of pre-emptive strike: get Them before they get Us. That, of course, is exactly the sort of bewitching that Tolkien warned most strongly against—the frenzy to solve a problem through one hubristic stroke, to grab the One Ring of power for oneself, even if that grabbing guarantees one's own fall into darkness.

A better vision is needed. The Council of the West must do its duty, to Christians, to Jews, and to the need of the world for peace. Having agreed that Israel must survive, within the protective ambit of Christendom, the council could engage Muslims—who are, themselves, in the process of restoring the Caliphate [rulership of Islam]—in a grand summit. Only then, when West meets East, in diplomatic twain, might a chance exist for an enduring settlement. When all Christians, and all Muslims, are brought to the bargaining table, they all become stakeholders in a pacific outcome.

This summit of civilizations would be difficult and expensive, even heartbreaking. It might take a hundred years. But let us begin because the reward could be great: blessed are the peacemakers.

The Knights of the West

With great effort, the West could unite around the Shire Strategy, seeking to secure and protect all our Christendom, spanning oceans and continents. But it won't be easy. It will take more than diplomacy—it will take strength.

This Shire is ours now, but the way things are going, it won't be ours permanently. So we must vow to defend the Shire, always. In the last of the "Rings" films, Aragorn the Strider proclaims, . . . , "A day may come when the courage of Men fails, when we forsake our friends and break all bonds of fellowship, but it is not this day. An hour of wolves and shattered shields when the Age of Men comes crashing down, but it is not this day! This day we fight! By all that you hold dear on this good earth, I bid you stand, Men of the West!"

We in the West will always need warriors. We must have *chevaliers sans peur et sans reproche*—"Knights without fear and without reproach"—to safeguard our marches and protect our homes. Men such as Leonidas, whose Immortal 300 held off the Persians at Thermopylae in 480 BC, long enough for other Greeks to rally and save the nascent West. Or Aetius, the last noble Roman, who defeated Attila the Hun, Scourge of God, at Chalons in AD 451. Or Don Juan of Austria, who led the Holy League to naval victory over the Turks at Lepanto in 1571. Or Jon Sobieski, whose Polish cavalry rescued Vienna from the Turks in 1683.

These are not just legends, not just fictional characters—they were real. And if we dutifully honor those heroes, as heroic Men of the West and of Christendom, we will be rewarded with more such heroic men.

Future epics await us. Future Knights of the West, ready to defend Christendom, are waiting to be born, waiting for the call of duty. If we bring them forth with faith and wisdom and confidence, then also will come new heroes and new legends.

Maybe it was meant to be. And that is an encouraging thought.

> *"Christianity and Islam, seen as the only two proselytizing faiths in the world, remain pitted against each other in a struggle for ascendancy, driven by presentiments of world glory and domination."*

Islamic and Christian Doomsday Scenarios Both Undermine Peace

Farzana Hassan

Farzana Hassan is a writer and activist who heads the progressive Muslim Canadian Congress. In the following viewpoint, she argues that conflicts between Christianity and Islam are fueled by religious differences. She notes that apocalyptic prophecies in both the Christian and Islamic traditions, and especially popular interpretations of these prophecies, encourage visions of expansive victory and reduce the possibilities of peace.

As you read, consider the following questions:

1. Why does Hassan say that Israel questions the Palestinian right of return?

Farzana Hassan, *Prophecy and the Fundamentalist Quest: An Integrative Study of Christian and Muslim Apocalyptic Religion.* Copyright © 2008 Farzana Hassan by permission of McFarland & Company, Inc., Box 611, Jefferson, NC 28640. www.mcfarlandpub.com.

2. What does Hassan give as two examples of ways in which fundamentalists have infiltrated politics?

3. According to Hassan, who is the Mahdi in Islamic prophetic thought?

The world has always been riddled with pockets of conflict: ethnic disputes, linguistic wars, and religious skirmishes simmer in limited areas around the globe. In recent years, however, a far broader and more ominous cloud has emerged over the length and breadth of the earth as a battle between the adherents of its two largest religions: Christianity and Islam. Although the conflict between Christendom and the Muslim world is not in fact strictly religious, the battle over people's hearts and minds is nonetheless steeped in religious rhetoric, with both sides invoking scripture to validate their respective stances. Although the conflict encompasses many aspects, such as the fight for political control, access to economic resources and cultural supremacy, its irrefutable underlying religiosity makes it that much more complex and impervious to change. Deriving its inspiration and thrust from scriptural sources—whether the Bible, the Quran, or Hadith [narratives concerning the actions of the Islamic Prophet Muhammad] literature—the conflict has attained an unshakable sanctity in the minds of the faithful, as it purports to link itself with the Divine, with its concomitant associations with ultimate power, goodness and glory.

Religion Colors the Conflict

Some assert that the conflict is only political in nature and not religiously inspired. The Arab-Israeli conflict, for instance, is a war for territory, control and hegemony in the region. All these aspects are of course crucial, but the warring parties perceive themselves first as religious entities distinct from their adversaries. It is religious differences that are at the foundation of this political struggle. A more religiously homogenous Middle East might not have witnessed the kind of blood bath the holy land has endured for so long. These identities are further solidified as conflicts take longer to resolve. For example, Israel questions the Palestinian right to return [that is the right of Palestinians exiled during war with Israel to return to their homes inside Israel] because of fears that the country will lose its Jewish character or even be reduced to a state where Jews will once again become a minority—a scenario dreadful to both Israelis and Diaspora Jews. But religious people from among both Palestinians and Jews lay claim to the land based on their respective understanding of scripture. Many from other parts of the world who have no direct stake in the conflict have also aligned themselves with the main players on the stage of global conflict based on religious, political or economic affiliation.

To date, much has been written about biblical prophecy, but the western world has yet to be introduced to the dimensions and implications of Islamic prophecy. . . . Perhaps at times as graphic as the scenarios presented in the Book of Revelation or the eschatological predictions contained in Daniel, Hadith paints a vivid picture of future events that lends credence to the prophetic gifts of the old prophets and soothsayers of Islam. The implications are so palpable among the faithful that candid analysis is not only warranted, but has become crucial for understanding the dynamics governing relations between the two faiths.

Christianity vs. Islam

Christianity and Islam, seen as the only two proselytizing faiths in the world, remain pitted against each other in a struggle for ascendancy, driven by presentiments of world glory and domination. The hopefuls on either side wish to impose their brand of religious ideology on the rest of the world, either through force or through persuasion. Thus evan-

Muslim Apocalyptic Literature and the United States

The dominance of the United States in the modern world and the pervasiveness of its influence in the Middle East have given it a parallel prominence in Muslim apocalyptic writings. . . . Negative feelings about the United States are not lacking in modern Muslim apocalyptic literature. Sa'id Ayyub, one of the most prominent of Muslim apocalyptic writers, writes: "[The United States] is now the principal center for the Jews. History bears witness that the United States of America, which has been occupied in all areas by the beliefs of the Antichrist, is the chief enemy of Islam in every place."

David Cook,
Contemporary Muslim Apocalyptic Literature. *Syracuse, NY:*
Syracuse University Press, 2005, pp. 150–151.

gelism and *Tabligh* or *D'awa* (the propagation of the message of Islam) are viewed increasingly by adherents as legitimate means of acquiring more market space for their respective ideologies. With a literalist approach towards understanding scriptural precepts and prophecy, fundamentalism has emerged with full gusto within both Islam and Christianity, manifested in umbrella organizations and localized groups. These movements strive to achieve their utopian ideals by distributing literature and propagating their world view through all the latest media outlets. Through such means as the network of Madrassahs [religious schools] in Pakistan and the "televangelism" of the Christian Coalition in the United States, fundamentalist groups have also infiltrated politics in order either to gain direct control over seats of power or to influence policy through lobbying and interest groups.

Among the adherents of Islam there is a prevalent view that their faith will eventually prevail over others as a religious ideology. It is a belief embedded in both the Quran and Hadith and therefore deserves our attention as a subject of analysis. . . . I hope that an examination of these hitherto largely unexplored parallels [between Biblical and Islamic prophecies] will in some way engender a greater understanding of many of the current conflicts in our embattled world.

While investigating apocalyptic religion, I have drawn heavily from the popular commentaries on prophetic literature available on various websites. Such sites tend to represent popular rather than academic views. Popular belief determines the tide of religions and must be accounted for in any analysis of religious movements. . . . Though mainstream biblical and quranic scholarship will question many of the conclusions of these commentaries, the purpose of the current inquiry is to delve deep into the dynamics of the religion of the laity and how those dynamics shape religious movements. A case in point is the anticipated arrival of the Mahdi within Muslim apocalyptic thought. Though serious Islamic scholarship doubts the validity of the numerous Hadith predicting the advent of a "rightly guided one" who will redeem the world of Islam in the end times, Muslim masses seem to have embraced this notion and eagerly await his arrival. Similarly, although the considered opinions of many mainstream Bible scholars may be at variance with the opinions of authors like Tim LaHaye and Hal Lindsey [who present apocalyptic visions of the Rapture], these authors nonetheless wield considerable influence on the masses. . . .

Deeply entrenched religious ideologies that have emerged in recent times have complicated matters further. . . . The apocalyptic vision has manifested itself in evangelical and jihadist movements as part of an unshakable religious mindset.

Periodical and Internet Sources Bibliography

The following articles have been selected to supplement the diverse views presented in this chapter.

Joseph Chambers	"Getting Excited About the Millennium," *Rapture Ready*, October 8, 2010. www.raptureready.com.
David Cook	"Islam and Apocalyptic," Center for Millennial Studies at Boston University, n.d. www.bu.edu/mille/index.html.
Mike Di Paola	"Caring for Pets Left Behind by the Rapture," *BusinessWeek*, February 11, 2010. www.businessweek.com.
Anthony Gregory	"The Left and the Politics of Rapture," *The LRC Blog*, March 30, 2010. www.lewrockwell.com.
Gary North	"The Foreign Policy of 20 Million Would-Be Immortals," LewRockwell.com, July 19, 2003. www.lewrockwell.com/north/.
Peter A. Olsson	"Group Death Myths in Terror Cult Groups," *Journal of Psychohistory*, Winter 2007.
Godwill A. Paul	"The Carnage of Religious Cults: The Case of David Koresh and the Branch Davidians," *Relijournal*, May 17, 2010. http://relijournal.com.
James P. Pinkerton	"National Suicide," *The American Conservative*, December 5, 2005. www.amconmag.com.
B.A. Robinson	"Common Signs of Destructive Cults," ReligiousTolerance.org, July 10, 2008. www.religioustolerance.org.
Todd Strandberg	"Defending the Pre-Trib Rapture," *Rapture Ready*, n.d. www.raptureready.com.

OPPOSING
VIEWPOINTS®
SERIES

CHAPTER 3

How Might Humans Bring About Doomsday?

Chapter Preface

Many people argue that humans could bring about doomsday simply by reproducing. This argument goes back to Thomas Malthus, a 19th century British economist. Malthus argued that population tends to increase much faster than the food supply—or, as he put it, "The power of population is infinitely greater than the power in the earth to produce subsistence for men." Malthus concluded that when population outran food, the inevitable result would be a reduction of population through "misery and vice." Thus, for Malthus, overpopulation would eventually lead to disease, war, or some other more-or-less apocalyptic disaster which would serve to cut the number of humans back to a manageable level.

Malthus' prediction of an overpopulation disaster did not actually come to pass. Instead, the Industrial Revolution and innovations in agriculture insured that the food supply grew faster than the population, not slower. "The whole world has never come close to outpacing its ability to produce food," according to Donald G. McNeil, Jr. in a June 15, 2008, article in the *New York Times*.

While Malthus' predictions have not come true, many believe that his ideas remain relevant. For example, in a 1998 article on the Negative Population Growth website (www.npg.org), the sociologist William R. Catton, Jr. argued that Malthusian ideas should in the modern day be applied not just to food, but to all of the earth's resources. Thus, he says, "Food is not the only component of 'sustenance' for modern human living; industrialized human societies rely on continuing flows of many other resources, and a cessation of supply of any essential commodity can be devastating." Catton concludes that, "Mankind is not only depleting essential mineral stocks. We are also diminishing the plant and animal resources available to future human generations, and destroying biological buffers against the effects of global climate change. We are stealing from the human future." He worries that the Malthusian pressure on the environment may be a "grave threat to humans" in the 2000s.

Other writers have rejected Malthus' doomsday arguments. "No one is saying that we aren't facing serious, extremely grave problems," noted social historian Iain Boal in a September 11, 2007, article in *Counterpunch*. "What we are questioning is the millenarianism, the endism, you could call it. . . ." Boal argues that Malthusian ideas of scarcity bringing about doomsday are intended to convince people that the hardships caused by capitalism are necessary. He concludes that scarcity is not caused by Malthusian forces, but rather by "artifice and force" applied by those in power.

In the viewpoints that follow, different writers look at other ways in which humans may, or may not, bring about doomsday.

> "We might be faced with truly cata-
> strophic threats before the century is
> out, and to deal with them we need to
> change our way of thinking."

Large Hadron Collider Doomsday Fears Can Help Scientists Prepare for Real Dangers

Ian Sample

Ian Sample is science correspondent for the Guardian *and author of* Massive: The Hunt for the God Particle. *In the following viewpoint, he discusses fears that the Large Hadron Collider (LHC), the largest and highest-energy particle accelerator, will destroy the earth. Sample concludes that the LHC is harmless, but argues that worries about it may help lay the groundwork for assessing more realistic threats. He argues that scientists and governments need to set up procedures to objectively analyze doomsday threats and determine how to respond to them.*

Ian Sample, "Global Disaster: Is Humanity Prepared for the Worst?" *The Observer*, July 25, 2010. guardian.co.uk. Copyright © 2010 Guardian News and Media Limited. Reproduced by permission.

As you read, consider the following questions:

1. According to Sample, what were some ways in which individuals claimed that LHC might destroy the world?

2. According to Nick Bostrum, humans are doomed only to learn from what?

3. What does Richard Posner want to set up in order to deal with potential catastrophes?

Corridors are deserted. Office doors are locked. Laboratories are quieter than usual. It can mean only one thing: conference season is upon us and it's time for scientists to shut up shop and take to the road, if only for a few days.

Physicists Will Not Destroy the World

For more than a thousand physicists, the destination last week [July 2010] was the Palais de Congrès in Paris [France], an enormous 1970s construction of jutting concrete and angled glass. Until Wednesday, the centre will host one of the most eagerly awaited meetings on the scientific calendar. The International Conference on High Energy Physics (ICHEP) has an impressive track record as the place where new discoveries are announced, but this time around there is an extra buzz in the air.

This is the first year that physicists at the Large Hadron Collider (LHC) [the world's largest and highest-energy particle accelerator] at Cern, the European particle physics lab near Geneva [Switzerland], will join researchers from other laboratories in unveiling their latest results. Talks at the meeting will cover a vast range of topics, from the performance of the LHC and other accelerators to quirks of the laws of nature and the hunt for the Higgs boson, the elusive particle said to give mass to the building blocks of nature.

One topic that will definitely not be discussed, at least not seriously, is whether the LHC might just destroy the planet.

Thanks to a few vocal doomsayers and a run of unsuccessful legal cases, the exotic idea has become lodged in the public consciousness. It has probably done more to raise Cern's profile than anything in the laboratory's recent history.

Wild claims about the risks of the LHC received blanket coverage from the world's media in the run-up to the machine being switched on last year [2009]. The nature of the catastrophe took on several guises. We heard that a black hole might appear beneath the Swiss countryside and steadily devour the Earth. Maybe planet-crunching entities called "strangelets" could pop into existence and reduce our hospitable rock to a sizzling ball no wider than Lord's cricket ground. Or the universe might "collapse" into a more stable state, wiping out life here and anywhere else it might lurk in the process. . . . Each of these scenarios, and more besides, were argued by a small number of concerned individuals to be clear and present dangers to humanity.

The Large Hadron Collider is not the first particle accelerator to be framed as a doomsday machine. Particle physicists have been accused of gambling with the future of humanity since at least the 1950s, when forerunners of the LHC were being built. Mention world-ending scenarios to staff on the LHC, or its main competitor, the Tevatron at Fermilab near Chicago, and you can expect a roll of the eyes at best. Physicists have gone to great pains to explain why such fears are unfounded. The time could have been better spent by getting on with research.

Lessons from Doomsday

Scientists have good reason to be weary of fanciful speculation over the safety of their experiments, but some academics claim there are valuable lessons to be learned from the LHC experience, ones that could save us from more realistic catastrophes before the century is out. Nick Bostrom, director of the Future of Humanity Institute at Oxford University, says that ad-

vances in fields such as weapons technology, artificial intelligence and synthetic biology (which has already given
researchers the tools to create viruses from scratch) could lead
to what he calls "existential threats". These are catastrophes
that play out on an unprecedented scale, ones that have the
potential to bring an end to the human story, either by wiping
us out completely, or by "permanently and drastically destroying our future potential".

The creation of a lethal synthetic virus that kills on a global scale is but one potential risk that Bostrom highlights.
Breakthroughs in physics could lead to new weapons that increase the dangers of war, he says, while advances in computing could see the advent of machines that can improve their
own intelligence, and surpass that of humans. Even attempts
to manipulate the atmosphere to combat global warming
might backfire and trigger a global disaster.

Bostrom says the LHC should be seen as a test case, used
by society to learn how to deal with events and technologies
that may genuinely threaten our existence in the future. "So
far, we haven't done very well, but events surrounding the
LHC could stimulate us into getting our act together for next
time, when the threats need to be taken more seriously," he
says. "I think the danger from particle accelerators is extremely
small, but there will be other areas that will cause major existential risks and we need to learn how to deal with these situations in a rational way."

Existential threats are nothing new. Schoolchildren learn
that an asteroid strike wiped out three quarters of Earth's species 65m [million] years ago and promptly ended the reign of
the dinosaurs. There have been at least four other mass extinctions, each one the result of an epic natural disaster. The
point that intrigues researchers such as Bostrom is that society
is bad at identifying dangers such as these, and even worse at
preparing for them. In an essay published in the *Journal of
Evolution and Technology* in 2002, Bostrom expressed dismay

at how little research has been done on serious threats to humanity, writing: "There is more scholarly work on the life-habits of the dung fly than on existential risks." Little has changed since, he says.

A major sticking point, says Bostrom, is that humans are doomed only to learn from direct experience. Nuclear reactors were made safer after the Chernobyl disaster in 1986. The UN [United Nations] drew up plans for a tsunami warning system in the Indian Ocean a year after 230,000 people died from a devastating wave in 2004. Plans to bolster flood defences around New Orleans are still being thrashed out, five years after hurricane Katrina killed nearly 2,000 and left thousands more homeless [in 2005]. In each case, the risks were known, but they were only acted on after the event.

One Chance to Get It Right

"Our attitude throughout human history has been to experience events like these and then put safeguards in place," says Bostrom. "That strategy is completely futile with existential risks. By definition, you don't get to learn from experience. You only have one chance to get it right."

One approach that has been used to clarify the nature and extent of a potentially dangerous situation involves setting up a panel of experts who understand the relevant science well enough to make an informed risk assessment. In 1999, the US physicist John Marburger III was director of Brookhaven National Laboratory on Long Island, New York. The lab is home to a particle accelerator called the Relativistic Heavy Ion Collider. That summer, a puff piece on the machine in *Scientific American* magazine led to two letters that raised concerns over whether the machine might create a black hole or cause other untoward damage to the planet. Marburger immediately convened a panel of leading physicists to work through every doomsday scenario they could think of and assess the risk of them happening. The panel concluded the machine was safe after drawing on the fact that more violent particle collisions caused by cosmic rays slamming into planets, stars and clouds of dust and gas have occurred in nature for billions of years. At Cern, a similar safety review of the LHC, the construction of which had only just begun, reached the same conclusion.

The safety reviews at Brookhaven and Cern were largely public relations exercises. Governments never considered pulling the plug on either machine, and courts dismissed legal challenges that sought injunctions on the colliders. But the reviews highlighted what some perceived to be a shortcoming of scientific panels. They could be seen as highly partial: particle physicists ruling on the safety of particle accelerators might well have a vested interest in the projects going ahead.

Soon after the fuss broke, Francesco Calogero, an Italian physicist and former secretary general of Pugwash, an organisation that pursues ways to reduce threats to global security, championed an alternative way of deciding how risky an experiment might be. In a paper entitled, "Might a laboratory experiment destroy planet Earth?", he backed for a more adversarial approach to risk analysis. Instead of one panel of experts, there should be two. The first, the blue team, makes the case for the experiment's safety, while the red team does its best to emphasise the dangers. The two then come together and decide whose arguments are the most robust.

"It is not perfect, but I think it is the best strategy," says Calogero. "It overcomes any perceived vested interest and gives people the chance to point out arguments that are not watertight and what might go wrong."

Improving Oversight

Others argue that decisions over the fate of humanity are too important to be left to panels of scientists. Richard Posner, a US appeals court judge and author of the 2004 book *Catastrophe: Risk and Response*, wants an Office of Risk and

We Must Consider the Future of Humanity

We need realistic pictures of what the future might bring in order to make sound decisions. Increasingly, we need realistic pictures not only of our personal or local near-term futures, but also of remoter global futures. Because of our expanded technological powers, some human activities now have significant global impacts. The scale of human social organization has also grown, creating new opportunities for coordination and action, and there are many institutions and individuals who either *do* consider, or *claim* to consider, or *ought* to consider, possible long-term global impacts of their actions. Climate change, national and international security, economic development, nuclear waste disposal, biodiversity, natural resource conservation, population policy, and scientific and technological research funding are examples of policy areas that involve long time-horizons. Arguments in these areas often rely on implicit assumptions about the future of humanity. By making these assumptions explicit, and subjecting them to critical analysis, it might be possible to address some of the big challenges for humanity in a more well-considered and thoughtful manner.

Nick Bostrum, "The Future of Humanity"
in Jan-Kyre Bergolsen, Evan Selinger, and Soren Riis,
New Waves in Philosophy of Technology.
New York: Palgrave McMillan, 2009, p. 187.

Catastrophe set up in the White House. The office would be charged with identifying potentially dangerous technologies and calling in experts to inform its own risk assessments. "The problem right now is that no single government department takes responsibility for these kinds of situations," he says.

An international network of such offices could go a long way to improving global security, Posner says, but the idea is controversial. "Done well, it could be extremely valuable, but there are many ways it might end up being politicised or compromised," says Bostrom.

According to Robert Crease, head of philosophy at the State University of New York and author of the 2006 book *The Philosophy Expertise,* our best hope for surviving existential threats is to train scientists as best we can and trust them to police themselves.

"You don't want a committee of people who don't have expertise trying to review the expertise of people who do. That doesn't improve matters. As soon as you set up a committee, quarrels develop over who's a member, who's best and who has what hidden agenda. It's a disaster," he says.

"The optimal course of action, the best we can do, is to improve, in each discipline, the review panels and the institutions that guarantee expertise. It boils down to trust. We don't like to rely on it, but we do every day," he adds.

For physicists meeting in Paris this week, the focus will be on discoveries rather than doomsday scenarios, and for good reason. The fears raised over particle colliders such as the LHC belong firmly in the realm of science fiction. But there are important lessons to be learned from the LHC story that go beyond particle physics. We might be faced with truly catastrophic threats before the century is out, and to deal with them we need to change our way of thinking. Instead of waiting for disaster to strike before making life safer, we have to be one step ahead. Contrary to the doomsayers' fears, the LHC might help ensure the end is never nigh.

"*The Universe as a whole conducts more than 10 million million LHC-like experiments per second. The possibility of any dangerous consequences contradicts what astronomers see—stars and galaxies still exist.*"

Large Hadron Collider Doomsday Fears Are Unfounded

CERN

CERN is the world's largest particle physics laboratory, located near Geneva on the Franco-Swiss border. In the following viewpoint, the laboratory argues that the Large Hadron Collider (LHC) particle accelerator is not dangerous. The lab notes that the types of collisions which occur at LHC are common throughout the universe. If such collisions had world-destroying potential, then the earth and most other planets would have been destroyed long ago. CERN concludes that there is no threat that the LHC will produce black holes, supernovas, strangelets, or vacuum bubbles, and therefore no threat that the collider will destroy the earth or the universe.

CERN, "The Safety of the LHC," http://public.web.cern.ch/public/en/lhc/safety-en.html, 2008. Copyright © 2008 CERN. Reproduced by permission.

As you read, consider the following questions:

1. According to CERN, how many collisions has nature generated on earth in the past billions of years?

2. According to the viewpoint, what is a strangelet?

3. Why can runaway fusion reactions not be produced in nitrogen tanks inside the LHC tunnel, according to CERN?

The Large Hadron Collider (LHC) [the world's largest and highest-energy particle accelerator] can achieve an energy that no other particle accelerators have reached before, but Nature routinely produces higher energies in cosmic-ray collisions. Concerns about the safety of whatever may be created in such high-energy particle collisions have been addressed for many years. In the light of new experimental data and theoretical understanding, the LHC Safety Assessment Group (LSAG) has updated a review of the analysis made in 2003 by the LHC Safety Study Group, a group of independent scientists.

Cosmic Rays and Black Holes

LSAG reaffirms and extends the conclusions of the 2003 report that LHC collisions present no danger and that there are no reasons for concern. Whatever the LHC will do, Nature has already done many times over during the lifetime of the Earth and other astronomical bodies. The LSAG report has been reviewed and endorsed by CERN's Scientific Policy Committee, a group of external scientists that advises CERN's governing body, its Council.

The LHC, like other particle accelerators, recreates the natural phenomena of cosmic rays under controlled laboratory conditions, enabling them to be studied in more detail. Cosmic rays are particles produced in outer space, some of which are accelerated to energies far exceeding those of the

LHC. The energy and the rate at which they reach the Earth's atmosphere have been measured in experiments for some 70 years. Over the past billions of years, Nature has already generated on Earth as many collisions as about a million LHC experiments—and the planet still exists. Astronomers observe an enormous number of larger astronomical bodies throughout the Universe, all of which are also struck by cosmic rays. The Universe as a whole conducts more than 10 million million LHC-like experiments per second. The possibility of any dangerous consequences contradicts what astronomers see—stars and galaxies still exist.

Nature forms black holes when certain stars, much larger than our Sun, collapse on themselves at the end of their lives. They concentrate a very large amount of matter in a very small space. Speculations about microscopic black holes at the LHC refer to particles produced in the collisions of pairs of protons, each of which has an energy comparable to that of a mosquito in flight. Astronomical black holes are much heavier than anything that could be produced at the LHC.

According to the well-established properties of gravity, described by Einstein's relativity, it is impossible for microscopic black holes to be produced at the LHC. There are, however, some speculative theories that predict the production of such particles at the LHC. All these theories predict that these particles would disintegrate immediately. Black holes, therefore, would have no time to start accreting [increasing gradually] matter and to cause macroscopic effects [effects large enough to be seen by the unaided eye].

Although theory predicts that microscopic black holes decay rapidly, even hypothetical stable black holes can be shown to be harmless by studying the consequences of their production by cosmic rays. Whilst collisions at the LHC differ from cosmic-ray collisions with astronomical bodies like the Earth in that new particles produced in LHC collisions tend to move more slowly than those produced by cosmic rays, one can still demonstrate their safety. The specific reasons for this depend whether the black holes are electrically charged, or neutral. Many stable black holes would be expected to be electrically charged, since they are created by charged particles. In this case they would interact with ordinary matter and be stopped while traversing the Earth or Sun, whether produced by cosmic rays or the LHC. The fact that the Earth and Sun are still here rules out the possibility that cosmic rays or the LHC could produce dangerous charged microscopic black holes. If stable microscopic black holes had no electric charge, their interactions with the Earth would be very weak. Those produced by cosmic rays would pass harmlessly through the Earth into space, whereas those produced by the LHC could remain on Earth. However, there are much larger and denser astronomical bodies than the Earth in the Universe. Black holes produced in cosmic-ray collisions with bodies such as neutron stars and white dwarf stars would be brought to rest. The continued existence of such dense bodies, as well as the Earth, rules out the possibility of the LHC producing any dangerous black holes.

Strangelets, Vacuum Bubbles, and Monopoles

Strangelet is the term given to a hypothetical microscopic lump of 'strange matter' containing almost equal numbers of particles called up, down and strange quarks.[1] According to most theoretical work, strangelets should change to ordinary matter within a thousand-millionth of a second. But could strangelets coalesce with ordinary matter and change it to strange matter? This question was first raised before the start up of the Relativistic Heavy Ion Collider, RHIC, in 2000 in the United States. A study at the time showed that there was no cause for concern, and RHIC has now run for eight years,

1. Any group of six elementary particles having electric charges of magnitude one-third or two-thirds that of the electron, regarded as constituents of all hadrons.

searching for strangelets without detecting any. At times, the LHC will run with beams of heavy nuclei, just as RHIC does. The LHC's beams will have more energy than RHIC, but this makes it even less likely that strangelets could form. It is difficult for strange matter to stick together in the high temperatures produced by such colliders, rather as ice does not form in hot water. In addition, quarks will be more dilute at the LHC than at RHIC, making it more difficult to assemble strange matter. Strangelet production at the LHC is therefore less likely than at RHIC, and experience there has already validated the arguments that strangelets cannot be produced.

There have been speculations that the Universe is not in its most stable configuration, and that perturbations caused by the LHC could tip it into a more stable state, called a vacuum bubble, in which we could not exist. If the LHC could do this, then so could cosmic-ray collisions. Since such vacuum bubbles have not been produced anywhere in the visible Universe, they will not be made by the LHC.

Magnetic monopoles are hypothetical particles with a single magnetic charge, either a north pole or a south pole. Some speculative theories suggest that, if they do exist, magnetic monopoles could cause protons to decay. These theories also say that such monopoles would be too heavy to be produced at the LHC. Nevertheless, if the magnetic monopoles were light enough to appear at the LHC, cosmic rays striking the Earth's atmosphere would already be making them, and the Earth would very effectively stop and trap them. The continued existence of the Earth and other astronomical bodies therefore rules out dangerous proton-eating magnetic monopoles light enough to be produced at the LHC.

Other Aspects of LHC Safety

Concern has recently been expressed that a 'runaway fusion reaction' might be created in the LHC carbon beam dump. The safety of the LHC beam dump had previously been re-

Large Hadron Collider by Chris Madden.

viewed by the relevant regulatory authorities of the CERN
host states, France and Switzerland. The specific concerns expressed more recently have been addressed in a technical
memorandum by [R.] Assmann et al. As they point out, fusion reactions can be maintained only in material compressed
by some external pressure, such as that provided by gravity inside a star, a fission explosion in a thermonuclear device, a
magnetic field in a Tokamak, or by continuing isotropic laser
or particle beams in the case of inertial fusion. In the case of
the LHC beam dump, it is struck once by the beam coming
from a single direction. There is no countervailing pressure, so
the dump material is not compressed, and no fusion is possible.

Concern has been expressed that a 'runaway fusion reaction' might be created in a nitrogen tank inside the LHC tunnel. There are no such nitrogen tanks. Moreover, the arguments in the previous paragraph prove that no fusion would be possible even if there were.

Finally, concern has also been expressed that the LHC beam might somehow trigger a 'Bose-Nova' [a very small supernova-like explosion] in the liquid helium used to cool the LHC magnets. A study by [Malcolm] Fairbairn and [Bob] McElrath has clearly shown there is no possibility of the LHC beam triggering a fusion reaction in helium.

We recall that 'Bose-Novae' are known to be related to chemical reactions that release an infinitesimal amount of energy by nuclear standards. We also recall that helium is one of the most stable elements known, and that liquid helium has been used in many previous particle accelerators without mishap. The facts that helium is chemically inert and has no nuclear spin imply that no 'Bose-Nova' can be triggered in the superfluid helium used in the LHC.

> *"The United States government made a cool, composed, calculated decision that it could bring about a precisely-defined political aim by employing nuclear weapons as an act of war."*

Apocalypse Remains a Real Possibility as Long as There Are Nuclear Weapons

Tad Daley

Tad Daley is the author of Apocalypse Never: Forging the Path to a Nuclear Weapon-Free World, *Rutgers University Press, 2010. In the following viewpoint, he argues that the most likely scenario for nuclear disaster is not an accidental launch. Rather, he says, the most disturbing threat is a conscious launch of nuclear weapons by a nuclear power such as the United States. Daley argues that to eliminate this danger, the world must work actively to eliminate all nuclear weapons.*

Tad Daley, "The Greatest Nuclear Danger Today Is Not Countdown to Zero's Nuclear 'Accident' 'Miscalculation' or 'Madness.' The Greatest Nuclear Danger Today, Still, Like 65 Years Ago, Is Nuclear War," CommonDreams.org, August 9, 2010. Reproduced by permission of the author.

As you read, consider the following questions:

1. What quote from President John F. Kennedy is the movie "Countdown to Zero" based on, according to Daley?

2. What nuclear policy has China adopted but the United States refuses to adopt, according to Daley?

3. What did Robert Gates say on C-Span in regard to the use of nuclear weapons against Iran and North Korea?

Two weeks before the 65th anniversaries of the atomic bombings of Hiroshima and Nagasaki, followed just six days later by the end of the Second World War, Magnolia Pictures released a new film called "Countdown to Zero." It was made by some of the same people who made "An Inconvenient Truth," and the filmmakers unapologetically expressed the hope that it would change the game on nuclear disarmament much as their previous film did on climate change.

The Nuclear Sword

The film quite shrewdly bases its argument on a single sentence, uttered by President John F. Kennedy nearly half a century ago. In his first speech before the United Nations, on September 25, 1961, the president said, "Every man, woman and child lives under a nuclear sword of Damocles, hanging by the slenderest of threads, capable of being cut at any moment by accident, or miscalculation, or by madness."

(Damocles was a court sycophant to the 4th Century BC tyrant Dionysius II of Syracuse. When Dionysius invited him one day to come and sit on his powerful throne, Damocles noticed, to his horror, a deadly sword suspended directly above, point down, held only by a single strand of the hair of a horse. In this way, Damocles learned the truth about the life of a ruler in the ancient world—or, as JFK wisely discerned, the life of everyone in the nuclear age.)

"Countdown" then, quite persuasively, details how, nearly half a century later, those three nuclear dangers remain quite imminent. It reveals just how close both the United States and the Soviet Union came, more than once, to launching not just one, but perhaps 101 nuclear-tipped missiles—utterly by accident. (The filmgoer is left to guess the likelihood that we can dodge that particular nuclear bullet indefinitely in a world of nine nuclear-armed nations, with perhaps soon more.) It examines episodes like the Cuban missile crisis in 1962 (and others almost wholly unknown to the public), when miscalculation, misinformation, or misunderstanding brought us to the brink of a civilization-ending nuclear war. (The filmgoer can perform the same exercise here.) And it illuminates just how many efforts have already been made, by non-state terrorists, to obtain or build a nuclear weapon, transport it to a major world city, and set it off—and just how likely it is that, eventually, somebody is going to pull that off.

Another Hiroshima

However, "Countdown" neglects to mention a fourth scenario by which the actual detonation of nuclear weapons might come about sometime in the next century, or the next decade, or the next year. Don't get me wrong. The film is excellent, especially as a vehicle for growing the nuclear disarmament movement, and preaching beyond the choir. This is a sin of omission, not commission. But during this week when we commemorate the 65th anniversaries of Hiroshima, Nagasaki, and the end of the Second World War, one is compelled to point out that the scenario the film omits is, ironically, another Hiroshima. Another Nagasaki. Another conscious, intentional launching of a nuclear weapon. Another calm, sober initiation of nuclear war.

Hiroshima and Nagasaki, which were instantaneously obliterated by the American atomic bombs "Little Boy" and "Fat Man" on August 6th and 9th, 1945 (devices perhaps a hun-

Moving Towards No First Use

The forthcoming US Nuclear Posture Review [2009] should include a thorough cost-benefit assessment of movement toward a no-first-use declaratory policy. Such an assessment should broaden the traditional focus of such policy reviews on deterrence 'requirements' and also include an analysis of how US nuclear declaratory policy influences the likelihood of nuclear proliferation, the consequences of proliferation, and perceptions of the illegitimacy of nuclear terrorism. Strategic logic and evidence suggest that a US no-first-use doctrine would have fewer costs and bring greater benefits than commonly recognised. Serious diplomatic issues remain to be addressed, especially how best to consult with NATO [North Atlantic Treaty Organization] and other allies and how to encourage other nuclear-weapons states, particularly the Russian Federation, to reduce their reliance on nuclear weapons. The seriousness of these concerns, and the best strategies for addressing them, cannot be determined in the abstract, without an assessment of the benefits of doctrinal change. A more thorough and broader analysis within the government of no-first-use policy is well overdue.

Scott Sagan, "The Case for No First Use,"
Survival, *vol. 51, June–July 2009, p. 178.*

dred times less powerful than many of the nuclear weapons deployed in arsenals today), were not, of course, atomic attacks carried out by the "madness" of non-state terrorists. Nor were they "accidents." Nor were they "miscalculations." The White House was not in a panic in August 1945. The orders to dispatch the B-29's carrying the atomic bombs were not issued in error. President Harry S. Truman and his advisors were not rushed into hurriedly deciding that if we didn't immediately launch a nuclear attack upon the Japanese, Tokyo would launch a nuclear attack (or, indeed, any kind of an attack) on us.

No, the United States government made a cool, composed, calculated decision that it could bring about a precisely-defined political aim by employing nuclear weapons as an act of war.

And that kind of nuclear eventuality, today, may be at least as likely as the three others described in "Countdown to Zero."

After the end of the Cold War, and before its corpse had even grown cold in the grave, the [Bill] Clinton Administration astonishingly chose not to diminish, but instead to expand the role of nuclear weapons in American national security doctrines. Now these weapons were designated for the first time as "counterproliferants." They were to be used not only in retaliation, but as a tool of pre-emption against "rogue states" and non-state actors. And they were to [be] used to prevent them from acquiring not only nuclear weapons, but chemical weapons and biological weapons as well.

The [George W.] Bush Administration, in its Nuclear Posture Review of December 2001, specifically articulated several scenarios where the United States might employ America's vast nuclear arsenal. Like the Clinton doctrines, many of these would be carried out not only not in response to a nuclear attack, but indeed not in response to any attack upon us at all. The Bush document even named seven particular states as the possible targets of a preemptive American nuclear attack upon them.

The [Barack] Obama Administration, in its Nuclear Posture Review of April 2010, stated plainly that it anticipated far fewer contingencies where the United States might actually use its nuclear weapons in combat. However, many nuclear policy experts had urged the new Administration to adopt an explicit policy of "No First Use"—a statement that our country would never employ nuclear weapons except to retaliate for the use of nuclear weapons against our allies or ourselves. China, despite laughably less powerful military forces than the United States, both conventional and nuclear, has long maintained such a policy of "No First Use."

But President Obama refused. His Administration insists that still, in certain circumstances, the president of the United States might need to authorize an American nuclear first strike. His Administration explicitly maintains the policy option for America to start a nuclear war.

In addition, for at least the past half decade, speculation has run rampant that either the United States or Israel, or both, might launch a preemptive attack on all elements of the Iranian nuclear complex, to forestall the (hypothetical future) possibility that Iran might someday obtain a nuclear arsenal of its own. Just this month, on Sunday August 1, [2010] the lead article in the *Washington Post* Sunday Outlook section, by Steven Simon and Ray Takeyh, was called, "A Nuclear Iran. Would America Strike to Prevent It?"

Preemptive Nuclear Strikes

Such a preemptive strike, of course, might be undertaken exclusively with conventional military forces. Or, it might not.

In the April 17, 2006 issue of the *New Yorker* magazine, investigative journalist Seymour Hersh alleged that to prevent Iran from acquiring nuclear weapons perhaps 5-10 years down the road, Pentagon [US military] planners were preparing not just military strikes on that country, but nuclear strikes. In the July 10, 2006 issue, Hersh reported that after lengthy and heated internal military debates, the Pentagon brass had concluded that, for the time being, a nuclear attack on Iran would be "politically unacceptable." But then on January 7, 2007, the

Times of London reported that Israel had begun laying the groundwork for a series of nuclear strikes on the Iranian nuclear infrastructure—perhaps utilizing tactical nuclear weapons supplied by the United States, and perhaps too in conjunction with American forces. If all that were not worrisome enough, in a CNN presidential debate on June 5, 2007, no less than four of the Republican presidential candidates indicated that to forestall a nuclear Iran, they would consider launching an American nuclear first strike against Iran.

But that all took place during the last Administration [of George W. Bush], right? Right. But in the press conference announcing the Obama Nuclear Posture Review on April 6, 2010, Secretary of Defense Robert Gates, asked directly about "No First Use," said that the Administration was unwilling to "limit ourselves so explicitly." And when asked directly about Iran and North Korea, he said that despite the limitations on American nuclear employment doctrines in the new document, with regard to those two states in particular, "all options are on the table." Live on C-Span. Three separate times.

Accident. Miscalculation. Madness. The creators of "Countdown to Zero" are quite correct in asserting that these contemporary nuclear perils are quite real, and, indeed, that they could come to pass today "at any moment." But all the nine nuclear-armed nations must also embrace the principle that nuclear weapons can serve no purpose other than to deter the use of nuclear weapons by others (a purpose that will disappear if, someday, we can achieve at last universal nuclear disarmament). The nuclear-armed nations cannot continue to conjure contingencies for employing nuclear weapons on any hypothetical field of battle, or to fantasize that starting a nuclear war could ever serve either their own national interests or the interests of the human community. If they do continue to do so, then we may just be on a countdown not to nuclear zero, but to something else nuclear entirely.

After all, said President Kennedy, in the very next sentence he uttered after his "nuclear Damocles" at the United Nations on September 25, 1961, "The weapons of war must be abolished, before they abolish us."

| "The bomb, in other words, is too often
seen as an absolute weapon, when it is
nothing of the sort."

Nuclear Apocalypse
Is Not Likely

Gerard DeGroot

*Gerard DeGroot is a history professor at the University of St.
Andrews in Scotland and the author of* The Bomb: A Life. *In
the following viewpoint, he reviews John Mueller's* Atomic Obsession. *Mueller's book argues that nuclear weapons are not
apocalyptically dangerous. They are not, he says, as devastating
as they are usually claimed to be, and they are very unlikely to
be used. DeGroot concludes that fear of nuclear weapons is more
dangerous than nuclear weapons themselves, and that nuclear
apocalypse is very unlikely to ever occur.*

As you read, consider the following questions:

1. According to Mueller, why might there be an ironic
   logic to allowing North Korea to go ahead with its
   nuclear program?

2. Mueller notes that the destruction of Hiroshima and
   Nagasaki were no worse than what?

Gerard DeGroot, "Dismissing Doomsday," *Arms Control Today*, November 2009. Reproduced by permission.

3. What does DeGroot say is the biggest fault of Mueller's book?

Every year, I teach a course on the atom bomb. At the end of each semester, I ask my students to tell me at what point the world came closest to nuclear Armageddon. The answers are usually predictable: the Cuban missile crisis [a confrontation between the Soviet Union, Cuba, and the United States in October 1962], the Yom Kippur War [a 1973 conflict between Israel and a Coalition of Arab states], the Indo-Pakistani conflict [a 1971 military conflict between Pakistan and India]. One year, however, I got a very different response.

It came from a student who was sitting in the far corner. Usually taciturn, he now looked ready to explode. "Thomas," I asked, "do you have something to offer?" He hesitated, then spat, "NEVER! There's never been a nuclear crisis. Nuclear weapons are stupid, and no nation would ever be stupid enough to use them."

Nuclear Weapons Are Stupid

At the time, I dismissed the outburst as heartfelt but wrong. Someone had clearly not been doing his homework. Now, however, after reading John Mueller's *Atomic Obsession*, I am not so sure. Mueller, professor of political science at Ohio State University, has provided lucidity and logic to my student's tirade. As Mueller argues, nuclear weapons are indeed stupid, and because they are, the risk of their use is tiny. Mueller's argument seems at first recklessly glib, but by the end of the book, I found myself swayed by his devastating logic. This is one of those annoyingly convincing books that undermine one's sacred truths. I am supposed to be an expert on this subject, but right now, I am questioning a lot of what I know. I may have to rethink my bomb course.

Mueller's thesis, as his title suggests, is that we are held captive by a paralyzing obsession when it comes to all things nuclear. That obsession corrodes common sense, causing us to lose our sense of proportion. Take, for instance, the present [2009] crisis in North Korea. The fact that atomic weapons and ballistic missiles are being tested [by North Korea] reduces otherwise sensible people in Washington [D.C.] to trembling panic. As Mueller indicates, the White House has, at various times in the recent past, seriously considered going to war to stop the North Korean project. Yet, such a war, experts predict, would result in a catastrophic loss of human life.

Would such a sacrifice be justified in order to prevent one nation from joining the nuclear club? Mueller shouts a resounding "no." So far, he argues, the North Koreans have tested devices of pathetically low yield. As for their missiles, they have only managed to demonstrate a capacity to hit the Pacific Ocean. These meager results have been achieved amid insolvency and mass starvation. It is clearly beyond the capacity of the North Koreans to develop their nuclear capability to a point where they could genuinely threaten any other nation. As the sometimes mischievous Mueller indicates, given the crippling cost of a nuclear program, there might even be ironic logic in allowing North Korea to go ahead because that seems the best way to bankrupt the vile regime of Kim Jong Il [North Korean dictator].

Mueller dismisses as bogus the risk of North Korea transferring weapons, material, or technology to other countries. The safeguards against such an eventuality, he believes, are simply too strong. In any case, he argues, given the depths to which North Korea's reputation has sunk, it seems unlikely that any state would risk universal opprobrium by making a Faustian deal with such a pariah. That seems, however, a bit like whistling in the dark, given that Syria has already made such a deal and Iran has also apparently cooperated with North Korea on missile development. Mueller takes solace in the assumption that provenance would be easy to trace, and guilt—not to mention punishment—would thus be shared.

Bang for the Buck

Suppose instead that Kim had invested his money in conventional weapons and traditional methods of delivery. The huge sums spent on his atomic project to date would have bought a lot of bombs and a fair number of bombers to drop them. Bombers, we need to remind ourselves, remain the most dependable method of delivering a payload. Failing that, the money could have been invested in heavy artillery because Seoul and other major cities in South Korea are easily within range. Had Kim taken either of these routes, he would have made his country a much greater threat to regional stability than it is now. One suspects that hardly anyone would have protested.

The bomb, in other words, is too often seen as an absolute weapon, when it is nothing of the sort. The term "absolute weapon" originated with Bernard Brodie's book by that title and has been treated as gospel ever since.

In impressively methodical fashion, Mueller dismantles the myths of an omnipotent leviathan. The imaginary monster, he feels, was brought into being by J. Robert Oppenheimer, who could not resist indulging in apocalyptic imagery after witnessing the first atomic test on July 16, 1945. "I am become Death, Destroyer of Worlds," he mused, quoting from the Bhagavad Gita [Hindu scripture]. Making a dent in the New Mexico desert or even leveling a few square miles of Hiroshima is not, Mueller insists, the same as destroying a world. By pretending that it is, we misjudge the threat the bomb poses.

A sense of proportion is essential. Mueller rightly points out that the destruction of Hiroshima and Nagasaki was no worse than the firebombing of Tokyo. The difference lay only in efficiency: one bomb achieved what elsewhere took thousands. We are constantly bombarded with grisly photographs of Hiroshima as proof of the bomb's awesome power, but photographs of Tokyo, although rarely displayed, show virtually identical destruction. In other words, nuclear weapons are not uniquely terrible. The bomb is unique in delivering potentially lethal radiation, but that too, Mueller argues, has been exaggerated. The horror lies in war, not in the specific methods of waging it.

Granted, the bombs dropped on Hiroshima and Nagasaki had yields of around 20 kilotons, while weapons today are often measured in megatons. That would suggest that it is facile to compare atomic weapons with conventional bombs. Mueller answers that rebuttal rather cleverly. There are indeed thermonuclear weapons capable of immense destruction, but they remain in the stockpiles of powers unlikely ever to use them, at least not as a first strike. The weapons causing the most fuss in the world at the moment, namely those possessed by Pakistan or being developed by Iran or North Korea, are similar in size to the Hiroshima bomb or even smaller.

The danger posed by these weapons, Mueller argues, is minuscule. He bases his argument on classical deterrence—a dwarf nuclear power such as Iran will forever be prevented from using its weapons by the knowledge that, if it did so, the nuclear giants would deliver vengeance a thousand times greater. Granted, nuclear retaliation might not be certain, but the risks are too great to allow the leader to gamble. The basic principle that once kept the United States and U.S.S.R. [Soviet Union] from destroying each other still stands: no leader, no matter how unstable he might seem, would ever take action that might result in the utter destruction of his country.

Some readers might find cold comfort in the shield of deterrence. While reading this book, I occasionally felt uneasy about Mueller's clinical logic, given that some world leaders are far from logical. That said, an argument could be made that nuclear weapons have forced leaders, even notoriously unstable ones, to act rationally. Some critics might argue that President Mahmoud Ahmadinejad of Iran cannot be trusted to act rationally, but it is equally possible that the bomb will impose sanity on him. A case in point, Mueller argues, is

China, a country once rather contemptuous of human life. In the 1960s and 1970s, China was in every sense a "rogue nation." Yet, it never came close to using its nuclear weapons, despite Chairman Mao Tse-tung's febrile boasts that he was prepared to allow one-half of his population to die in defense of communism.

Sowing Fear

Rather predictably, the Mueller train of logic moves relentlessly to the conclusion that Iran and North Korea should be allowed to pursue their nuclear projects. He sees the two nations as akin to spoiled children who will probably find that the toy they covet is not quite so attractive if it is granted without need of a tantrum. Clearly, the value of these weapons for Ahmadinejad and Kim lies not in their potential for devastation but in the abhorrence they inspire in the rest of the world. Once the weapons cease to sow fear, they lose their value as a tool of political extortion. Mueller also argues that the best way to insure that proper safeguards are applied to Iranian or North Korean weapons is to treat those nations like responsible members of the nuclear club. Although Mueller does not advocate simply abandoning all efforts to persuade Iran and North Korea to abstain, he insists that persuasion must remain in the realm of responsible dialogue. Threats of military action, he insists, will only encourage greater stubbornness. If a nation is labeled a rogue, it tends to behave in that manner.

The word "if" does not, however, juxtapose comfortably with kiloton power. As [former Secretary of Defense] Robert McNamara once argued, "[A] strategic planner . . . must prepare for the worst plausible case and not be content to hope and prepare for the most probable." That explains why it was considered necessary for the United States to spend $5.5 trillion on nuclear weapons between 1940 and 1996. The same logic suggests that the best way to keep Iran from using an atomic bomb is to prevent it from ever making one. Thus, Secretary of State Hillary Rodham Clinton has maintained that Iran must be prevented from getting the bomb "at all costs." What does that mean? Would prevention be worth another war in the Middle East, one that would probably be even more destructive than the current conflict in Iraq? Mueller, an expert at keeping things in perspective, rightly points out that the danger of going to war with Iran and further inflaming Islamic opinion is far greater than the danger that could ever be posed by an Iranian nuclear weapon.

Mueller also does not grant much credence to what he calls the "cascadologists," namely those so-called security experts who maintain that an Iranian or North Korean bomb would trigger relentless proliferation. As he points out, cascadologists have been crying wolf ever since the Soviets first exploded a nuclear weapon in 1949. If warnings uttered decades ago had proven correct, there would be about 40 nuclear powers today. Instead, most nations have proven remarkably reluctant to join the nuclear club, and some have even suspended their membership by getting rid of their weapons. This reluctance can be explained by the fact that the weapons have no military utility and are ferociously expensive. Even Libyan leader Moammar Gaddafi eventually came to the conclusion that nuclear weapons are "crazy."

Mueller rejects entirely the notion that the bomb is a tool of coercion, useful in frightening adversaries into doing what is wanted. As he points out, the fact that the United Kingdom had nuclear weapons did not prevent Argentina from invading the Falklands. Israel's possession of atomic bombs did not frighten off the Egyptians on Yom Kippur in 1973; Israel would have been better off buying tanks. "The United States," he adds, "possesses a tidy array of thousands of nuclear weapons and for years has had difficulty dominating downtown Baghdad [capital of Iraq]—or even keeping the lights on there."

Questioning Sacred Truths

Like a marksman at a fairground shooting gallery, Mueller carefully guns down the sacred truths of nuclear orthodoxy. "All radiation is dangerous." Bang! "Atomic weapons were essential to the stability of the Cold War." Bang! The ducks keep coming, and Mueller keeps shooting them down. He eventually arrives at essentially the same conclusion many arms control advocates have long advanced, namely that nuclear weapons should be abolished. He comes to that conclusion, however, from a very different direction. In his view, the weapons should go not because they are dangerous, but because they serve no purpose.

Mueller sees nuclear weapons as a massive misjudgment inspired by irrational fear. Worst-case scenario fantasists have exercised an iron grip on international sensibilities, he argues, forcing nations to spend money on weapons that they did not need. In the aftermath of the September 11 [2001, terrorist] attacks, that same fear has prompted an obsession with nuclear terrorism, a danger Mueller also judges bogus. Addicted to fear, the doomsday merchants have turned to the terrorist because Russia could no longer provide a fix. The last section of his book aims at this new bogey, blowing it away with the same deadly precision. Central to Mueller's argument is the assertion that terrorists are basically opportunists: they achieve success by keeping attacks simple. The complexity of a nuclear strike—the time, effort, risk, and expense—contradicts that ethic.

In examining the terrorist scenario, Mueller analyzes the process of funding, designing, building, transporting, and detonating a weapon and breaks the process down into 20 clearly identified tasks. As he stresses, the terrorist needs to succeed at each task, while those who wish to stop him require only one success. Even the very generous 50–50 odds that he gives for each stage in the process mean the accumulated likelihood of success is less than one in a million. Examined through that lens, a decision to pursue nuclear weapons seems ludicrous. It makes no sense for a terrorist organization to invest huge sums of money, time, and effort in such a risky enterprise because its purpose can be served much more easily by strapping a few pounds of gelignite to the body of a fanatic and sending him into a crowded train. For these reasons, Mueller is not greatly concerned by reports that [terrorist organziation] al Qaeda has been seeking nuclear material and information for bomb-making.

Obsession and Armageddon

Lurking ominously in our nuclear consciousness is the specter of Armageddon, a terribly inappropriate word that warps good sense. In popular perception, a nuclear explosion has wrongly come to be equated with the apocalypse. That in turn has demanded preparation for the worst-case scenario. Stripped of our sense of proportion, we cower in an artificial world of absolute danger, imprisoned by our fears. The steps we have taken to protect ourselves from an exaggerated danger are arguably more destructive than the danger itself, as has been potently demonstrated in Iraq.[1]

Mueller's achievement deserves admiration even by those inclined to resist his central thesis. The book is meticulously researched and punctuated with a dry wit that seems the perfect riposte to the pomposity of security experts who have so far tyrannized debate. Although by no means the last word on nuclear weapons, Mueller deserves praise for having the guts to shout that the atomic emperor has no clothes.

The biggest fault of the book is the way he attacks one obsession with another. He is clearly passionate about his topic, and that passion causes him to overplay his hand. For instance, the contention that radiation is less dangerous than we

1. The United States invaded Iraq in 2003 on the grounds that the country was building nuclear weapons. No nuclear weapons were found, but the US occupation was costly and became very unpopular.

think is not necessary for his central argument. Likewise, his attempt to bring the destruction of Hiroshima into perspective seems occasionally callous. His insistence that atomic weapons are not as dangerous as they seem could easily be used by those prepared to think the unthinkable, those who have occasionally tried to construct scenarios in which nuclear weapons might conceivably be used. After all, deterrence is strengthened by a belief in Armageddon, even if that belief occasionally warps good sense.

This still very worthy book deserves attention and discussion. Its publication coincides nicely with a renewal of tension in Iran's relations with the rest of the international community. Despite that inadvertent plug, I doubt the book will do very well, for the simple reason that, as Mueller admits, "ghoulish copy very commonly sells" while serene good sense does not. "Nothing is as boring as a book about how urgent something isn't," he says. Boring or not, and it is not, the book should nevertheless be packaged up and sent to Presidents Barack Obama and Nicolas Sarkozy [of France] and Prime Minister Gordon Brown [of Britain] with a simple message: "Please calm down." While reading *Atomic Obsession*, I constantly heard President Franklin Roosevelt whispering, "The only thing we have to fear is fear itself."

In his preface, Mueller wryly remarks that he wants his book to be a cure for insomnia. He sees no reason to suffer sleepless nights worrying about a danger that does not exist. The book does indeed have a soporific [sleep-inducing] effect, not through dry prose but through devastating logic. Since reading it, I have felt a tiny bit better about the world my children will inherit.

> *"If we wait forty or fifty years before taking serious action, the die will have been cast and a thousand generations of our descendants will have to live with the consequences of the climate we bequeathed them."*

Global Warming Will Cause a Planetwide Catastrophe

R.T. Pierrehumbert

R.T. Pierrehumbert is a professor in geophysical sciences at the University of Chicago. In the following viewpoint, he argues that global warming is a dangerous threat. He notes that human emissions are significantly increasing carbon dioxide levels in the atmosphere. There is evidence that this may cause a major and devastating climate shift. Pierrehumbert also notes that because carbon dioxide stays in the atmosphere for a very long time, future generations will have to suffer with the consequences of our decisions. He concludes that the world needs to address the problem of carbon dioxide emissions and climate change immediately to avoid catastrophe.

R.T. Pierrehumbert, "Climate Change: A Catastrophe in Slow Motion," *Chicago Journal of International Law*, vol. 6, Winter 2006, pp. 1–8. Reproduced by permission of The University of Chicago Law School.

As you read, consider the following questions:

1. What does Pierrehumbert say makes global warming unique in the four billion year history of the planet?

2. Pierrehumbert says that carbon dioxide is implicated in virtually all of the great climate shifts in Earth's history, including what?

3. How does Pierrehumbert explain the precautionary principle?

The word catastrophe usually brings to mind phenomena like tsunamis, earthquakes, mudslides, or asteroid impacts—disasters that are over in an instant and have immediately evident dire consequences. The changes in Earth's climate wrought by industrial carbon dioxide emissions do not at first glance seem to fit this mold since they take a century or more for their consequences to fully manifest. However, viewed from the perspective of geological time, human-induced climate change, known more familiarly as "global warming," is a catastrophe equal to nearly any other in our planet's history. Seen by a geologist a million years from now, the era of global warming will probably not seem as consequential as the asteroid impact that killed the dinosaurs. It will, however, appear in the geological record as an event comparable to such major events as the onset or termination of an ice age or the transition to the hot, relatively ice-free climates that prevailed seventy million years ago when dinosaurs roamed the Earth. It will be all the more cataclysmic for having taken place in the span of one or a few centuries, rather than millennia or millions of years.

The End of Nature

Humans have become a major geological force with the power to commit future millennia to practically irreversible changes in global conditions. This is what [author and environmentalist] Bill McKibben refers to as "The End of Nature." As an example of the impact life has on global climate, the imminent global warming caused by humans does not stand out as unique or even unusually impressive. When oxygen-generating photosynthetic algae evolved between one and two-and-a-half billion years ago, they changed the composition of one-fifth of the atmosphere, poisoned much of the previous ecosystem, and more or less terminated the dominant role of methane as a greenhouse gas (oxygenation also, to be fair, set the stage for evolution of multi-celled organisms—the animals and plants we know and love). And when plants colonized land half a billion years ago, they vastly increased the rate at which atmospheric carbon dioxide is converted to limestone in the soil, leading to severe global cooling. One hardly wants to contemplate the kind of environmental impact statement that would have to be filed for either of these innovations.

What makes global warming unique in the four billion year history of the planet is that the causative agents—humans—are sentient. We can foresee the consequences of our actions, albeit imperfectly, and we have the power, if not necessarily the will, to change our behavior so as to effectuate a different future. The conjuncture of foresight and unprecedented willful power over the global future thrusts the matter onto the stage where notions of responsibility, culpability, and ethics come into play. The philosopher Hans Jonas finds in this "imperative of responsibility" a need for a fundamentally new formulation of ethics—one that takes greater cognizance of future generations and of the biosphere at large. It is against this backdrop that the foundation of international institutions capable of dealing with the catastrophe of global warming must be seen.

Carbon Dioxide

In this section I will review the basic physical features that make global warming fundamentally different from all other

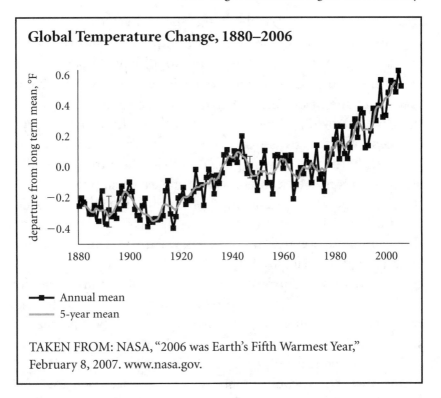

Global Temperature Change, 1880–2006

- Annual mean
- 5-year mean

TAKEN FROM: NASA, "2006 was Earth's Fifth Warmest Year," February 8, 2007. www.nasa.gov.

pollution problems faced by humans. The problem of ozone destruction by chlorofluorocarbons (the "ozone hole" problem) was a small warm-up act sharing some characteristics with the global warming problem. But because the ozone hole problem was somewhat more limited in scope, and abatement of chlorofluorocarbons did not force society to confront any really difficult economic decisions, it is in a qualitatively different class. Human-induced emissions of several gases other than carbon dioxide also contribute to global warming, but in the long run, carbon dioxide is by far the biggest player and the most embedded in economic activity. I will thus restrict my discussion to this gas alone.

Carbon dioxide is present only in very low concentrations in the atmosphere. Immediately before the beginning of the industrial era, you would have needed to sift through a million molecules of air to find 280 molecules of carbon dioxide.

If all of the carbon dioxide in the atmosphere were gathered together into a layer near the ground, the layer would be about two meters deep. Most of us would have to stand on a chair to breathe. It is because there is relatively little carbon dioxide in the atmosphere that human economic activity has the prospect of doubling its concentration within the twenty-first century, with greater increases in sight thereafter. It would be much harder for anything we do to significantly change the atmosphere's oxygen content, which makes up about a fifth of the atmosphere. Despite its low concentration, carbon dioxide plays a key role in determining the Earth's climate because this gas greatly retards the efficiency with which the planet loses energy to space by infrared (heat) radiation. The major constituents of the atmosphere are essentially transparent to infrared radiation. Carbon dioxide warms the Earth in the same way a sleeping bag or down comforter warms a person—by reducing the rate of heat loss. For the Earth, this additional blanketing allows the planet to maintain a higher temperature than would otherwise be possible, given the rate of solar energy input from the Sun.

Water vapor is the other major player in the Earth's energy budget, but its concentration in the atmosphere is buffered on a time scale of weeks by the huge oceanic reservoir of water, which can rapidly evaporate into the atmosphere and equally rapidly rain out. Water vapor thus adjusts in response to other changes in climate (principally temperature); rather than being a prime mover, it is a feedback amplifying other causes of climate change, including carbon dioxide increase. . . .

Carbon dioxide, in contrast, has a very long lifetime in the atmosphere and very weak natural sources; therefore, changes in the rate at which carbon dioxide is put into the atmosphere have great leverage over the atmosphere's carbon dioxide content. Carbon dioxide is implicated in virtually all of the great climate shifts in Earth's history, including the coming and going of the Ice Ages; the eons of warm ice-free states that the dinosaurs lived in some seventy million years ago; the collapse of the Earth into a globally frozen state in the Neoproterozoic era some six hundred million years ago; and the maintenance of conditions favorable to life on the very young Earth, when the Sun was much fainter than it is today. We know from Earth's history that carbon dioxide has an enormous impact on the habitability of our planet, but history also humbles us by revealing major gaps in our understanding of the nature and severity of the impact. For a geologist, the idea of doubling the atmosphere's carbon dioxide concentration is outright terrifying, akin to closing one's eyes and spinning a thermostat dial that has not been touched in a long time, and without even the benefit of knowing quite whether it is a gas furnace or a hydrogen bomb at the nether end of the thermostat's wires.

Unprecedented Change

The unique character of the challenge posed by carbon dioxide pollution derives from a triad of properties. First, human-induced emissions of carbon dioxide constitute a huge disturbance of the natural carbon cycle, causing changes in the atmosphere's carbon dioxide concentration that are large and of unprecedented speed in the annals of geological history. In the absence of fossil fuel burning, the natural carbon dioxide level is maintained by volcanic activity, specifically an escape of about five hundred million metric tons of carbon per year into the atmosphere from the Earth's interior. Fossil fuel burning currently puts about fifteen times this amount into the atmosphere annually, and the rate is increasing exponentially. As a result, the atmospheric carbon dioxide level has already increased from its pre-industrial value of 280 molecules per million to a present value of 370 molecules per million, and this level is expected to reach twice the pre-industrial value before the end of the current century. By way of comparison, carbon dioxide concentration during the two million years prior to the industrial era, encompassing the entire history of the human species, had fluctuated between a low of 180 molecules per million during the Ice Ages and a high of about 300 molecules per million during the inter-glacial periods. One has to go back perhaps ten million years to find another time when the carbon dioxide concentration was as high as we will make it during the next century. Looking a little further into the future, fossil fuel burning could quadruple the pre-industrial concentration within four hundred years under a business-as-usual scenario. This is comparable to the values that climate modelers use to reproduce the steamy, ice-free climate of the Cretaceous that existed some seventy million years ago. To turn back the climate clock seventy million years in the course of a few centuries is not a thing to be undertaken lightly.

Second, the expected changes in temperature caused by the increase of carbon dioxide are of a direction and magnitude unprecedented in the past two million years. During that time, the climate has fluctuated from a maximum global mean warmth approximating values prevailing around 1950 to temperatures about six degrees colder during the major Ice Ages. Simulations of global mean warming associated with a doubling of carbon dioxide lie in the range of two to four degrees Centigrade, with no guarantee that the higher figure truly represents the worst possible case. At the high end of this range, we are talking about a climate change two-thirds as big as the transition to an ice age but with this important difference: the expected warming would be added on top of the maximum temperatures experienced in the past two million years. Therefore, we have no natural analogues to tell us how the complex web of physical and biological interactions would respond to such a drastic climate change. We are driving into unknown territory, and, given the present imperfect state of physical and especially ecological simulations, with a windshield heavily encrusted with mud.

Third, and most significant, the excess carbon dioxide we put in the atmosphere today is removed exceedingly slowly, meaning that the carbon dioxide we emit in the next half century will alter the climate for millennia to come; even if we wholly ceased using fossil fuels after fifty years, the harm could not be undone. The lifetime of carbon dioxide in the atmosphere is often mistakenly quoted as being on the order of a hundred years; this figure is actually the result of a fallacious and largely meaningless method of aggregating the many physical processes that operate on widely differing time scales into a single number which is supposed to represent the amount of time some extra added carbon dioxide will stay in the atmosphere. The fact is that for each kilogram of carbon dioxide put into the atmosphere today, only a small portion will be rapidly absorbed into the ocean. After five hundred to one thousand years of slow uptake by the ocean, fully a quarter of that kilogram will remain in the atmosphere. A portion of that will be taken up by the ocean over the next ten thousand years by slow processes related to ocean sediments, but fully 7 percent of our initial kilogram will stick around for hundreds of thousands of years. It has been estimated that fossil fuel exploitation could eliminate the natural ice age cycle for the next half-million years, with presently unforeseeable consequences for the storing and catastrophic release of exotic methane-bearing ices in the ocean. The long reach of our actions over the eons gives us unprecedented power over the future, and with that power comes unprecedented responsibility.

The Poles and the Tropics

An innocuous-sounding two to four degree Centigrade increase in average global temperature carries along with it much larger regional changes in temperature and precipitation, which can in turn have profound consequences. Polar regions warm more than the average, and already, at the present early stage of warming, one-fifth of Arctic summer sea ice has disappeared. Arctic summer ice may be gone in fifty years, which will have dire consequences for polar bears and other marine mammals. The opening of arctic ports and shipping routes may well prove to be a boon for the market economy (as well as a source of political conflict and territorial disputes), but the increasingly intensive exploitation of the area is hardly likely to be good for natural ecosystems. We are learning, too, that land ice can respond more rapidly to climate than previously thought. The Greenland summer melt zone has expanded dramatically and many of the Greenland glaciers are surging into the ocean. At the opposite pole, the Larsen B ice shelf in the Antarctic has collapsed for the first time in ten millennia. The success of the documentary film *March of the Penguins*, a straightforward account of a year in the life of the Antarctic's emperor penguins, is a testament to the deep affinity people feel for these brave creatures. Emperor penguins adapted over millions of years to life on the ice. Their life cycle is intimately tied up with the long inland march along sea ice and shelf ice, undertaken to protect their newborns from oceanic predators. The penguins would struggle mightily to undo ten million years of evolution in a century.

In the tropics, temperature changes little in the normal course of the year. How will the Amazon ecosystem respond to the extensive warming and drying predicted by some models? Warm water holds less oxygen than cold water. Throughout the world, then, global warming will stress sensitive freshwater fish living in shallow streams; coastal saltwater shellfish will likely also be affected by the heat. Agricultural diseases, human diseases, and parasite infestations (including potato blight, bark beetles, West Nile, and malaria) can expand their range with warming. Summer heat waves will become more severe, placing particular stress on places that are already barely tolerable during the summer. Some regions will experience extensive droughts, and if the monsoons should cease, the results will be catastrophic for countries such as India. Also, hurricanes draw their energy from warm water, so the intensity (and perhaps also the number) of hurricanes is likely to increase in the future. There are indications that the expected increase in the destructive power of hurricanes is already underway. The impact in low-lying coastal regions may be exacerbated by a sea level rise even greater than currently forecast, if glaciers should prove more responsive to temperature increases than conventionally thought.

Dangerous Possibilities

Major ocean circulations are also likely to change, with uncertain consequences for the Earth's climate and its oceanic ecosystems. Carbon dioxide becomes an acid when it dissolves in water; the resulting acidification of the ocean will make it harder for coral to form their skeletons. While carbon dioxide in the air acts as a fertilizer for many kinds of plants, meaning that an increase in its concentration could have limited beneficial effects on agricultural plants, this increase could also have adverse and unexpected consequences for land ecosystems (just as dumping phosphate and nitrate fertilizer into the Gulf of Mexico has not proved beneficial for the environment).

In addition, historical evidence shows that the climate system has abrupt switches built into it, and that climate changes in fits and starts rather than along a smooth, gentle curve. Notwithstanding the movie *The Day After Tomorrow*, this does not mean that global warming risks bringing on an ice age. Rather, what we risk is a switch to a climate that has much more dramatic swings in it from one decade to the next, making adaptation much more difficult. The last ten thousand years, which embrace the entire history of civilization, have had an unusually steady climate, and we are uncertain about what it would take to disrupt this happy state of affairs.

Many of the above impacts are in the realm of the possible rather than the probable, and it is presently difficult to say how large such impacts would be, or even how probable they are. However, a cogent case has been made that one should pay more attention to low-risk but potentially catastrophic events, as opposed to the current focus on the "most probable" case. Those who would sneer that such an application of the "precautionary principle" would lead to paralysis are relying on an extreme caricature of the principle that has little resemblance to the way it is used in practice. For example, if one is thinking about driving down a mountain road at night and has faulty headlights, knows that the ravine ahead has a rickety bridge over it, and has heard that there has been a storm that may have washed the bridge away, one would be quite justified in driving slowly or perhaps even postponing the trip, even if it was not known for certain that the bridge had been swept away. No doubt, those who disdain the "precautionary principle" would be quite happy to load their whole family in the car and put the pedal to the floor.

Running Out of Time

The global nature of the climate change problem has some novel policy implications and also creates some opportunities. The atmosphere is well-mixed with regard to carbon dioxide. From the standpoint of climate change, carbon dioxide released in Sydney, Australia is in every regard interchangeable with carbon dioxide released in Beijing, China or Edmonton, Canada. The atmosphere truly is a global commons with respect to carbon dioxide, making emissions trading schemes far more benign than would be the case for pollutants, such as mercury, which have locally lethal impacts. The harm caused by the emission of carbon dioxide in Edmonton is not felt primarily, if at all, in Edmonton. This scenario means that one is confronted with an especially severe form of the free rider problem. A particularly unstable situation is created when a major emitter like the United States perceives (foolishly) that it will suffer minimal harm from the impacts of climate change and perceives (also foolishly) that actions taken to reduce emissions will derail its economy.

Because of the extremely long-term impact of each additional year's carbon dioxide emissions, the calculus of delay is completely changed as compared to other pollution problems. Ordinarily, in the face of uncertainty, a certain amount of delay could be justified; technology improves so as to make abatement cheaper, and one could wait to get a peek at the growing impacts to see just how deleterious they actually are. For many kinds of pollution, bad decisions are, to some extent, reversible. For example, suppose that at some point society has decided that it can no longer afford stringent restrictions on particulate emissions by power plants. It holds to this decision despite the possibility that a rather modest rollback in tax cuts for the wealthy could easily cover the costs. Such a society, in essence, places a higher value on the ability of wealthy individuals to afford new Hummers than it does on the health of children and other vulnerable populations. A future generation with different values may ultimately have to live with the guilt of a large number of preventable deaths of children from asthma and other respiratory ailments. However, a feeling of guilt is all that future generations are burdened with since the adverse impacts will disappear within a few years of action taken by more enlightened leaders. We do not have even this dubious luxury with respect to global warming. If we wait forty or fifty years before taking serious action, the die will have been cast and a thousand generations of our descendants will have to live with the consequences of the climate we bequeathed them.

The problem of long-term consequences is compounded by the long lead time for developing new energy infrastructure and technology and by the long capital life—well over a half century—of newly built electric power plants. Invest-

ments being made today, investments that the coming generation will be reluctant to write down, are committing the world
economy to another half century of runaway carbon dioxide
emissions. We are, in fact, rapidly running out of time to act.

> "The data themselves—that is to say, actual observations of the earth's climate—are hardly grounds for much excitement."

Global Warming Doomsday Fears Are Exaggerated

Kevin Shapiro

Kevin Shapiro is a research fellow in neuroscience and a student at Harvard Medical School. In the following viewpoint, he argues that concerns about global warming are greatly exaggerated. He says that most doomsday scenarios are seriously overstated. He also points out that climate models are very uncertain, and that scientists do not really know how carbon dioxide in the atmosphere will affect climate change. He concludes that the furor over global warming has more to do with research funding and politics than with science.

As you read, consider the following questions:

1. Shapiro says that most of what we "know" about global warming comes from what?

Kevin Shapiro, "Global Warming: Apocalypse Now?" *Commentary*, September 2006. Copyright © 2006 by Commentary Inc. Reproduced by permission.

2. Why does Shapiro say that the makers of *An Inconvenient Truth* resorted to animation to show the plight of polar bears?

3. According to Shapiro, what is our best bet to avoid increased reliance on coal?

As early as 1896, [Swedish chemist Svante] Arrhenius had proposed that surface temperatures rise in proportion to atmospheric CO_2 [carbon dioxide], which absorbs radiated heat that would otherwise escape into space. Noting that CO_2 can be generated by the burning of coal, Arrhenius predicted that the growth of industry might eventually result in a warmer planet (in modern terms, this would be called "anthropogenic forcing")—a salutary outcome from a Scandinavian point of view, since a more temperate climate would likely be a boon to agriculture in the North.

The Greenhouse Effect

This "greenhouse effect" is the cornerstone of the contemporary notion of global warming. A hundred years after Arrhenius wrote, the concentration of CO_2 in the atmosphere has already nearly doubled, and the earth's surface is on average about 0.6°C [Celsius] warmer—enough to convince many scientists and laypeople that Arrhenius was right at least about this. In 2001, the official estimate of the Intergovernmental Panel on Climate Change was that we should expect a warming of about 3°C, give or take a few degrees, in the decades ahead.

But today's prophets of climate change are not quite so sanguine as Arrhenius about the prospect of anthropogenic forcing. This is because, according to some models, even a relatively small rise in global mean temperature would result in dramatic changes in local climate patterns. While climate modelers generally agree that farmers in subarctic latitudes will benefit from warmer summers and milder winters, their forecast for the rest of the planet approximates the apocalypse: famine, drought, hurricanes, floods, mass extinctions—the list goes on. Most of these calamities, said to be of such a scale that they could threaten the viability of human civilization, are predicted to result from changes in weather patterns that would follow from rising temperatures in the oceans and the lower atmosphere.

Scientific Consensus

The earth's climate is an extraordinarily complex system, and most climatologists would probably concur that local perturbations cannot be foretold with precision. But given the magnitude of the prospective problem, many pundits and policymakers—with the backing of the scientific establishment—have become less interested in improving our understanding of climate change than in pressing for an immediate solution. By this they mean somehow reducing (or at least stabilizing) the concentration of CO_2 in the atmosphere.

This is a difficult proposition, to say the least. About 70 percent of electricity in the United States is generated by the combustion of fossil fuels, mostly coal; our transportation network, which accounts for about a quarter of our greenhouse-gas emissions, is almost entirely dependent on petroleum. The picture in the rest of the world is not much better, as economic pressures dictate the construction of new coal-fired power plants not only in China and India but also in Germany and Eastern Europe. . . .

Nevertheless, as the intellectual class has increasingly become convinced of the reality of man-made climate change—recent [2006] "converts" range ideologically from Gregg Easterbrook of the liberal *New Republic* [magazine] to Ron Bailey of the libertarian *Reason* [magazine]—environmentalists have correspondingly stepped up their efforts to build public support for some sort of action. The media now regularly proclaim the impending reality of climate change and encourage alarm. ABC News, offering not so much as a bow toward a scientific approach, recently asked viewers to submit stories about "global warming" in their own communities. Even the July 2006 issue of *Condé Nast Traveler*, not generally known for coverage of science and technology issues, includes tips for travelers who feel guilty about the damaging emissions generated by their airplane flights.

Among the more serious efforts to sway the debate are two new books, Tim Flannery's *The Weather Makers: How Man Is Changing the Climate and What It Means for Life on Earth* and Elizabeth Kolbert's *Field Notes from a Catastrophe*, along with [former Vice President] Al Gore's much ballyhooed film, *An Inconvenient Truth*. Each of these presents a more or less-comprehensive view of the scientific case for global warming, and describes in vivid detail some of the changes already attributed to rising temperatures: melting permafrost in Alaska, the crack-up of the Larsen B ice shelf in Antarctica, thinning sea ice in the Arctic, fiercer and more numerous hurricanes in the Atlantic. And each suggests that the threat of global warming is supported by an overwhelming scientific consensus that, in their view, leaves absolutely no room for dissent.

The basic elements of the consensus are relatively easy to comprehend. Indeed, the three most important have already been mentioned. One is that surface thermometers have registered a global mean increase in temperature of about 0.6°C over the last century, give or take 0.15°C. This means that global temperatures are now higher than they have been in at least a thousand years, and perhaps since before the last major ice age. Likewise, atmospheric CO_2 has increased from preindustrial levels of around 250 parts per million by volume (ppmv) to around 378 ppmv, a level probably not seen since the Pliocene era, around 3.5 million years ago, when atmospheric CO_2 was higher for reasons that are basically unknown. There is little doubt, however, that at least some of the current increase is attributable to human activity.

Simulations to Prove Catastrophe

So much for the data. The rest of what we "know" about global warming comes from intricate computer simulations, called general circulation models (or GCM's), which make use of these data and innumerable other observations about the earth's atmosphere in order to predict the effects of continuing increases in CO_2. Almost all the models forecast more warming, with the amount depending on various assumptions built into them. Although it is not clear from these results exactly why we should be alarmed—more on this later—Kolbert, Flannery, and Gore do their best to make sure that we *are* alarmed, enough to be willing to take drastic action. Each of them takes a slightly different rhetorical tack, but the ultimate message is always the same: we are on the verge of a catastrophe.

Kolbert's book, which grew out of a series of articles written for the *New Yorker* in 2005, adopts a journalistic style; she reports from the "front lines," as it were, embedding her essential points in well-crafted vignettes and conversations with scientists. She treks to Alaska, where an expert in permafrost tells her that temperatures have already become dangerously high. In Greenland, she observes cracks and crevasses in the ice sheet, which seem to suggest that the island's glaciers are melting. Experts on mosquitos, frogs, and butterflies attest to ecological changes that similarly portend a warming earth. Some people, it seems, have already bitten the bullet: Kolbert describes how the Dutch are abandoning their 500-year-old battle against the seas, dismantling their dikes and designing floating houses. . . .

As compared with *Field Notes*, Tim Flannery's *The Weather Makers* is more flamboyant, more decisive, and far more belligerent. Flannery, an Australian zoologist and something of a scientific celebrity, does little to hide his contempt for those who fail to take the problem of climate change as seriously as he does.

The Weather Makers starts off on an encouraging note, with an acknowledgment that climate change is difficult to evaluate impartially because the scientific issues are bound up in competing political and economic interests. Unfortunately, this pretense of evenhandedness collapses by the first chapter, which introduces the Gaia hypothesis—roughly, the idea that the earth's oceans, soil, atmosphere, and living creatures function together as a kind of superorganism, resisting changes that would alter the global climate. It is our failure to adopt a Gaian view, Flannery suggests, that has led us into the current global-warming predicament. . . .

In Flannery's view, the "consensus" based on climate change models is too conservative. He thinks that climate change has already taken off in full force, and the outlook for the future is dire indeed. Where Kolbert is circumspect about warming trends at the poles, Flannery suggests that the entire polar ecosystem is on the brink of collapse, and that coral reefs bleached by overheated oceans may never recover. Droughts in the American West, Australia, and Africa are all attributed to global warming, as are Europe's recent heat waves and floods. And this is just the beginning: Flannery predicts a rapid rise in global temperatures that will wipe out innumerable animal and plant species, not to mention agriculture in much of the world. . . .

Flannery reserves his greatest ire for big business, and for the conservative politicians he sees as subservient to it. In the end, he seems to think that if we fail to break free of our captivity to "big oil" and "big coal," the imperative to regulate the climate will leave us with no choice but to submit to some sort of world government.

Worst-Case Scenarios and an Inconvenient Truth

Somewhere in-between Kolbert's measured warning and Flannery's hysterical fearmongering lies *An Inconvenient Truth*. Narrated in its entirety by Al Gore, the film is part documentary, part hagiography: ominous warnings about the threat of climate change are interleaved with flashbacks to Gore's childhood and other formative moments in the former Vice President's career.

The movie covers much of the same ground as *Field Notes* and *The Weather Makers*, but with less concern for factual accuracy. Gore all but explicitly blames global warming for the disastrous effects of Hurricane Katrina [August 2005]; even Flannery only goes so far as to offer Katrina as an example of the kind of disaster that *might* become more prevalent in a warming world, and climatologists themselves are divided over whether global warming implies an increase in tropical-storm activity. In another segment, an animated polar bear is shown swimming for his life in an ice-free Arctic sea. Presumably the filmmakers resorted to animation because, in fact, most polar-bear populations are not under such imminent threat.

Gore's overall strategy is to present the worst of worst-case scenarios as if they were inevitable, barring a miraculous reduction in atmospheric CO_2. He suggests, for example, that Greenland's ice cap is in danger of melting, which in turn would cause the jet stream to shut down—a bit like the scenario dramatized in the 2004 disaster film *The Day After Tomorrow*. Needless to say, most earth and atmospheric scientists consider the likelihood of such an event to be vanishingly low. Animated maps show sea levels rising to inundate Miami, New York, and Shanghai, which is more than even the most extreme predictions would seem to allow.

One might note that *An Inconvenient Truth* contains more than its share of ironies and curious lacunae [gaps]. Gore suggests that viewers can help cut back on their own carbon emissions by taking mass transit. And yet, during much of the movie, Gore is shown either riding in a car or traveling on a plane—by himself. He berates Americans for our reliance on fossil fuels, but, chatting amiably with Chinese engineers, seems peculiarly unconcerned by Chinese plans to build hundreds of new coal-fired power plants. Indeed, he compares vehicle-emission standards in the United States unfavorably with China's. Touting "renewable" fuels like those derived from biomass (which at present offer no carbon savings compared with traditional fuels), he does not mention nuclear power or other practical carbon-reducing alternatives to coal, oil, and gas. . . .

Does Gore have a point? Is it really true that the threat of climate change impels us to take action?

Unexciting Data

The data themselves—that is to say, actual observations of the earth's climate—are hardly grounds for much excitement. For example, the fact that global temperatures and CO_2 levels are correlated in the climatological record is not in itself cause for panic. Consider the "smoking gun" for many global-warming alarmists—the Vostok ice core, an 11,775-foot-long sliver of Antarctic ice that has allowed scientists to extrapolate atmospheric CO_2 and temperature anomalies over roughly the past 420,000 years, showing that temperature and CO_2 have risen and fallen roughly in tandem over this time frame.

But the key word here is "roughly." The Vostok data make it clear that at the onset of the last glaciation, temperatures began to decline thousands of years before a corresponding decline in atmospheric CO_2. This observation cannot be replicated by current climate models, which require a *previous* fall in CO_2 for glaciation to occur. Moreover, an analysis published in *Science* in 2003 suggests that the end of one glacial period, called Termination III, preceded a rise in CO_2 by 600

Move Slowly on Global Warming

Global warming is indeed real, and human activity has been a contributor since 1975.

But global warming is also a very complicated and difficult issue that can provoke very unwise policy in response to political pressure. In 2005, for instance, Congress clearly made a very bad decision about climate change when it mandated accelerated production of ethanol. Critics had argued then that corn-based ethanol would actually result in *increased* carbon dioxide emissions. An increasing body of science has since verified this position. . . .

Although there are many different legislative proposals for substantial reductions in carbon dioxide emissions, there is no operational or tested suite of technologies that can accomplish the goals of such legislation. Fortunately, and contrary to much of the rhetoric surrounding climate change, there is ample time to develop such technologies.

Cato Handbook for Policymakers, *7th ed.,*
Cato Institute, 2009, p. 475. www.cato.org/pubs/.

to 1,000 years. One explanation for this apparent paradox might be that global warming, whatever its initial trigger, liberates CO_2 from oceans and permafrost; this additional CO_2 might then contribute in turn to the natural greenhouse effect.

Should we worry that adding even more CO_2 to the atmosphere by burning fossil fuels could contribute to a runaway warming effect? Probably not. In simple physical terms, each extra unit of CO_2 added to the atmosphere contributes less to the greenhouse effect than the previous unit, just as extra layers of paint applied to a pane of glass contribute less and less to its opacity. For this reason, we have already experienced 75 percent of the warming that should be attributable to a simple doubling of atmospheric CO_2 since the late 19th century, a benchmark we have not yet reached but one that is frequently cited as dangerous by those who fear global warming. Moreover, it seems unlikely that we can do very much about it.

Most models, of course, predict much *more* warming to come. This has to do with the way they account for the effects of clouds and water vapor, which are assumed to amplify greatly the response to man-made greenhouse gases. The problem with this assumption is that it is probably wrong.

Many scientists who study clouds—including MIT's [Massachusetts Institute of Technology] Richard Lindzen, a prominent skeptic of climate-change alarmism—argue that the data show the opposite to be true: namely, that clouds act to limit, rather than aggravate, warming trends. In any case, the GCM's have failed miserably to simulate observed changes in cloud cover. Flannery, to his credit, is cognizant of this criticism, and acknowledges that the role of clouds is poorly understood. By way of a response, he draws attention to a computer simulation showing a high degree of correspondence between observed and predicted cloud cover for one model on a single day—July 1, 1998. Overall, however, GCM simulations of clouds are a source of significant error.

Indeed, the models are subject to so much uncertainty that it is hard to understand why anyone would bother to get worked up about them. Generally speaking, the GCM's simulate two kinds of effects on climate: natural forcing, which includes the impact of volcanic eruptions and solar radiation, and anthropogenic forcing, which includes greenhouse gases and so-called aerosols, or particulate pollution. But the behavior of most of these factors is unknown. . . .

To be sure, the business of fine-tuning GCM's provides a livelihood for many climatologists, and may one day yield valuable insights into the workings of the earth's climate. But the output of these models is hardly a harbinger of the end of civilization.

Not Science

If the empirical basis for alarmism about global warming is so flimsy, it is reasonable to ask what can account for the disproportionately pessimistic response of many segments of society.

Part of the problem is that global warming has ceased to be a scientific question—by which I do not mean that the interesting scientific issues have actually been settled, but that many of those concerned about global warming are no longer really interested in the science. As Richard Lindzen has reminded us, the Kyoto Protocol [a climate change agreement which entered into force in 2005] provides an excellent illustration. Although there is widespread scientific agreement that the protocol will do next to nothing to affect climate change, politicians worldwide continue to insist that it is vital to our efforts to combat the problem of global warming, and scientists largely refrain from contradicting them.

Some have suggested that the underlying reason for this is economic. After all, public alarm is a powerful generator of science funding, a fact that is not lost on theorists and practitioners. In 2003, the National Research Council, the public-policy arm of the National Academy of Sciences, criticized a draft of the U.S. National Climate Change Plan for placing too much emphasis on improving our knowledge about the climate and too little on studying the likely impacts of global warming—the latter topic being sure to produce apprehension, and hence grants for more research. By the same token, the Kyoto process seems to lumber on in part because of the very large number of diplomats and bureaucrats whose prestige and livelihoods depend on maintaining the perception that their jobs are indispensable.

Money aside, it may be that many scientists have a knack for overinterpreting the importance of their own work. It is of course exciting to think that one's research concerns an unprecedented phenomenon with far-reaching political implications. But not only can this lead to public misperception, it can encourage a politicization of the scientific literature itself. Scientists skeptical of the importance of anthropogenic warming have testified that it is difficult to publish their work in prestigious journals; when they do publish, their articles are almost always accompanied by rebuttals.

In fact, the scientific "consensus" on climate change—at least, as it is summarized by Gore, Flannery, and the like—includes a very large number of disparate observations, only a small number of which are pertinent to understanding the actual determinants of contemporary climate change. The fact, for example, that certain species have become scarce or extinct is frequently presented as a cause for alarm about the climate. But such ecological shifts are often the result of idiosyncratic local conditions, and in any case are largely irrelevant to the broader issue of global warming. . . .

Political Truths

The really curious element here is that many of those who seem to have become convinced of the reality of climate change appear rather unwilling to take meaningful steps toward cleaner sources of energy. Like Flannery, they simply assert that a carbon-free economy will somehow be much more efficient and productive than one powered by fossil fuels—because, of course, we will be rid of evil and greedy energy companies, which many alarmists suspect are at the root of the problem.

Practically speaking, however, they have little to offer. Very few Democratic politicians have advocated the construction of new nuclear-power plants, a key element of the [George W.] Bush administration's energy plan and probably our best bet to avoid an increased reliance on coal. Although Senator Edward M. Kennedy (among other Democrats) signed a bill that would require the U.S. to derive 20 percent of its energy from renewable sources by 2020, he has strenuously opposed a wind farm planned off the coast of Cape Cod, visible from his Hyannisport [Mass.] family estate.

The overall effect of these inconsistent policy goals—limiting fossil-fuel consumption without activating any viable substitutes—will be to drive up the price of energy, a move that will probably not much affect the affluent but will be quite problematic for the rest of us. Al Gore will be able to continue to crisscross the country by jet, while feeling virtuous about having encouraged the shift worker to reduce his energy consumption by using public transportation. And if the problem of global warming does not eventuate, so much the better. Alarmists will be able to reassure themselves that they have forestalled a catastrophe, even if this comes at considerable expense to the economy as a whole.

There are many good reasons to wean ourselves from a dependence on fossil fuels, not least to cease enriching unsavory regimes in places like Saudi Arabia, Iran, and Venezuela. But in combating climate change, we should not ignore the damage done by the proponents of global-warning themselves in diverting money and energy away from more obvious and well-substantiated problems. Unfortunately, many people seem to be more concerned with the supposed menace of global warming, about which we can realistically do very little, than with problems like infectious disease, about which we can do quite a bit. Speaking of inconvenient truths, this is a real one.

> "Let us not forget that each seed that we have stored inside that seed vault has the potential . . . to save the world."

The Doomsday Seed Vault Can Help Prevent a Global Warming Catastrophe

Lars Peder Brekk

Lars Peder Brekk is the Norwegian Minister of Agriculture and Food. In the following viewpoint, he discusses the Svalbard Global Seed Vault, which stores crop seeds. He argues that the vault is vital to preserve genetic crop diversity, especially given the devastating environmental changes that may result from global warming. He also argues that more money must be invested in plant breeding to increase genetic diversity. He concludes that the seed bank will potentially help to save the world.

As you read, consider the following questions:

1. According to the viewpoint, who is Tay Gipo?

2. The International Treaty on Plant Genetic Resources for Food and Agriculture established common rules for what, according to Brekk?

Lars Peder Brekk, "One Year Anniversary Seminar of the Svalbard Global Seed Vault," Rejeringen.no, February 26, 2009. www.rejeringen.no. Reproduced by permission.

3. Brekk says that we cannot solve the global challenges of climate change, poverty reduction, and food security by leaving food production to whom?

It is with great pleasure that I welcome you to the Svalbard Global Seed Vault[1] First Anniversary Seminar. I am especially honoured by the positive response that all of you have given to our invitation to this seminar by travelling thousands of kilometres—in fact, more than 2000 kilometres NORTH OF OSLO [Norway]—to join us on this beautiful exotic arctic island.

Conserving Diversity

Last year, when we invited [guests] to the opening of the Seed Vault, we were more than gratified with the worldwide attention that the official opening received. It affirmed our feelings—

That the Seed Vault is a monumental achievement.

That it demonstrates the increase in understanding of the critical importance of crop diversity.

And, that all it takes is a few practical steps, with all of us working together, and we can contribute to the conservation of that diversity.

But beyond the physical presence of those hundreds of thousands of individual seeds that now fill the shelves of the Seed Vault, we in the Norwegian Ministry of Agriculture and Food invited our partners to co-host this anniversary seminar because we believe that the Seed Vault should and can continue to inspire others about the vital importance of crop diversity. . . .

Right now, our world faces an unprecedented challenge—a challenge that threatens the quality of life on every continent. I am talking about climate change—

1. The Seed Vault stores seeds so they will be preserved in case of disaster. It is located on the Norwegian island of Spitsbergen.

As science tries to keep up with the looming threats of changing climates and weather patterns, increasing temperatures and melting ice caps, we here in Svalbard are well aware that the most important use of crop diversity in the coming decades will be helping agriculture adapt to these changes.

This meeting is not just about conserving plant genetic resources.

And it is not just about climate change and its causes and impacts.

It is about how climate change will affect agriculture; how the world can use plant genetic resources to be prepared.

One year ago, when the Svalbard Global Seed Vault was officially opened, this room was filled with more than 150 invited guests representing 33 countries and 5 continents. . . .

But at this moment, I would like to mention another person who was present that day. One of the most memorable voices of that seminar. Mr Tay Gipo—a subsistence farmer from the Philippines. Mr Gipo only had four years of school— four years of formal education—but he also was blessed with thousands of years of local agricultural know-how that was passed down to him from village elders.

Bordagol Seeds

Like other rice growers in the Philippines, Mr Gipo switched to high-yielding, improved varieties in the late 1960s. But, he and his neighbours still struggled with pests and diseases, like the tungro virus. During a particularly tough year, he noticed one plant in his field that did not succumb to the virus. He literally had to pull the plant from the mouth of a farm animal who was planning to have it for a snack—he saved the seeds, replanted them and the next season he harvested 25 kilograms just from the seeds of that one plant. With his incredible success, the rice he himself named "Bordagol" was born. He shared his success by sharing his seeds with his neighbors. The word spread and, in spite of his lack of educa-

The Seed Vault Opens

Bored into the middle of a frozen Arctic mountain . . . , the [Svalbard Global Seed] vault's goal is to store and protect samples of every type of seed . . . in the world.

As of Thursday [February 2008], thousands of neatly stacked and labeled gray boxes of seeds—peas from Nigeria, corn from Mexico—reside in this glazed cavelike structure, forming a sort of backup . . . , in case natural disasters or human errors erase the seeds from the outside world.

Elisabeth Rosenthal,
"Near Arctic, Seed Vault Is a Fort Knox of Food,"
New York Times, *February 29, 2008. www.nytimes.com.*

tion, he was invited to join a research institute where he learned rice breeding and improved his "Bordagol", increasing its yield and resilience and therefore increasing the yields of the other farmers in his area.

I mention his name for two reasons. One to illustrate how the field-level knowledge of our farmers continues to be the most important element of crop conservation. But also to keep his memory alive. Because just days ago we received word that our fellow agriculturalist, Tay Gipo, passed away this month at the age of 64.

His legacy remains in the fields of the Philippines—where his "Bordagol" is grown by his neighbours—and their neighbors. And his legacy remains here is Svalbard where seeds of his "Bordagol" are safely stored for the future.

When he spoke here last year, he ended his talk by asking—and then answering—a question that obviously was on his mind when he made his Odyssey to Svalbard—he asked how the Seed Vault would help him and his family. He answered it himself—frank and straightforward—he said—"I don't know. I don't know if it will."

I call upon all of us in this room, and countless others who have been involved in this process at all of its levels—the gene banks, the plant breeders, the international organizations, the research institutions, the governments—to remember his question.

Because, his answer was in many ways the correct one:

- No one knows if the Seed Vault ever will be needed.

- No one knows if and when the seeds will be sent back to their depositor to restore a seed collection that has been lost.

- That's how insurance policies work.

- Even if it turns out that the insurance pay-off will never be needed, that policy still has incredible importance, because we know we are protecting something of extremely high value.

When we opened the Svalbard Global Seed Vault last year, each guest was invited to help carry a box of seeds into the seed vault. That was the first deposit on our insurance policy—and those seeds are still there, a line of defence against whatever the future may hold.

I will invite all of you to do the same later today to celebrate our Seed Vault's first year. And you too will be contributing to our global insurance policy.

Because the ominous fact of the global situation is undeniable—we are losing crop diversity—diversity that is crucial for the world's food security.

A Response to Climate Change

Agriculture depends on the diversity of plant and animal genetic resources, and on their ability to adapt to change. As we face climate change, all of us in the global community need to dedicate ourselves to initiatives to preserve and ensure sustainable use of these resources—initiatives like the Seed Vault.

This means massive efforts by both developed and developing countries.

This means increasing investments in agriculture. In 2008, the World Bank's World Development Report turned a corner in recognizing that the agricultural sector must be placed at the centre of the development agenda.

This means recognizing the importance of sustainable management—not just of crop diversity, but also of forests, of seas and inland waters, of livestock.

It is the macro picture of globalization and the micro reality of conservation—one crop, one tree, one animal, one fish at a time. These challenges can be met, and they must be met.

At the macro level, I call your attention to the International Treaty on Plant Genetic Resources for Food and Agriculture that now has been signed by 119 nations. It is a compelling example of what can be achieved through collaborative action. The Treaty establishes common rules to make crop diversity freely accessible and to ensure that any benefits derived from that access are shared.

The Treaty recognizes farmers' rights—the contribution to the conservation and development of crop diversity that has taken place in the fields of farmers like Tay Gipo and his neighbours over the millennia—farmers who still use local crops in traditional agricultural systems.

Trade is another area I want to mention, where the links to both climate change and food security are undeniable. The Uruguay Round Agreement on Agriculture stated quite firmly that all Members needed to make commitments to non-trade concerns and specifically mentioned food security and the need to protect the environment. This is a thought that should guide our future work. We cannot solve the global challenges of climate change, poverty reduction and food security by leaving food production to a handful of powerful exporters. It is increasingly important, and acknowledged, that all countries should maintain an appropriate level of self sufficiency.

Seeds to Save the World

By expressing his uncertainty; Mr Gipo also expressed the notion that until now, gene banks, have been a "secret" treasure. Who outside of the small community of plant geneticists understood the importance of collecting, cataloguing and conserving our agricultural heritage—a heritage that is also our future food supply? I do not think it is so secret anymore! I think the Svalbard Global Seed Vault has raised understanding and awareness: that we must—and we will—protect crop biodiversity in order to feed a warming world.

Of course Mr Gipo was not sure whether he—as a subsistence farmer—would ever benefit from access to genetic resources. After all, he was the end of a chain coming from Svalbard, from the gene banks, from the plant breeders, from the seed dealers. Mr Gipo might also have been concerned for his future ability to produce and sell his own locally adapted rice varieties on the local markets.

Norway believes that to give positive answers to the kinds of challenges the hundreds of millions of other farmers like Mr Gipo are facing, it is necessary to be pro-active. In fact, last year at the opening seminar, my predecessor Mr. Riis-Johansen announced that Norway would set up an annual contribution to the benefit-sharing fund of the International Treaty, starting in 2009—a contribution from the Norwegian Ministry of Agriculture and Food equal to 'point one percent' of the value of all agricultural seeds that are sold in Norway.

Well, it is now 2009—and just before I left for this meeting, I authorized our first contribution to the fund. For Norway, this fund represents the most direct way to increase the ability of developing country farmers to improve, conserve and utilize the crops in their fields—and of course to feed their families.

New and improved seed must be produced if we will stand ready to face climate change and overcome food-insecurity. Storing seeds here at Svalbard is necessary, but not enough. We simply must improve financing of plant breeding in developing countries. With our contribution, we expect to increase the focus on plant breeding activities in developing countries with a special attention on the interest of poor farmers.

I want to emphasise that the challenges we face can only be met through our joint efforts. Climate change and food insecurity are closely linked, and hence our policies must reflect this reality and be mutually supportive. The sustainable management of our resources will serve to mitigate the effects of climate change but sustainable management also must be seen as the most critical pre-requisite for development.

My hope is that we during this seminar, by using the crop diversity as a springboard to explore both issues of climate change and food security and the practicalities of making society act in good time, together will examine the ways in which long-term action can be made politically and practically acceptable when short-term thinking prevails. . . .

To sum up, I return again to Mr Gipo. It was his friends and neighbors who convinced him he should name his special rice. He chose the name Bordagol. Bordagol it turns out is the name of a cartoon character—one with the ability to save the planet. Let this be a reminder to all of us about why we are here today. We don't know when. We don't know where. But let us not forget that each seed that we have stored inside that seed vault has the potential to do just that—to save the world.

| "Can the development of patented seeds for most of the world's major sustenance crops . . . ultimately be used in a horrible form of biological warfare?"

The Doomsday Seed Vault May Lead to Biowarfare Disaster

F. William Engdahl

F. William Engdahl is a journalist and the author of Seeds of Destruction: The Hidden Agenda of Genetic Manipulation. *In the following viewpoint, he argues that the Doomsday Seed Vault at Svalbard may be a dangerous plot. He argues that investors in the seed vault have a history of imperialistic use of genetically modified crops. He also says that investors like the Rockefeller Foundation were involved in eugenics research attempting to eliminate non-Aryan groups in the 1920s. Engdahl concludes that the seed vault may be connected to genetic biowarfare research. Such research, he says, may have apocalyptic consequences.*

F. William Engdahl, "'Doomsday Seed Vault' in the Arctic," *Global Research*, December 4, 2007. Copyright © 2007 F. William Engdahl, Global Research. Reproduced by permission of the author.

As you read, consider the following questions:

1. According to Engdahl, what did the declining yield characteristic of hybrids mean for farmers who used the new Green Revolution seeds?

2. How does Engdahl define "Terminator" seed technology?

3. What did Epicyte develop in 2001, according to Engdahl?

When Bill Gates [Microsoft founder and philanthropist] decides through the [Bill and Melinda] Gates Foundation to invest some $30 million of their hard earned money in a project, it is worth looking at.

Millions in a Seed Bank

No project is more interesting at the moment than a curious project in one of the world's most remote spots, Svalbard. Bill Gates is investing millions in a seed bank on the Barents Sea near the Arctic Ocean, some 1,100 kilometers from the North Pole. Svalbard is a barren piece of rock claimed by Norway and ceded in 1925 by international treaty.

On this God-forsaken island, Bill Gates is investing tens of his millions along with the Rockefeller Foundation, Monsanto Corporation, Syngenta Foundation and the Government of Norway, among others, in what is called the 'doomsday seed bank.' Officially the project is named the Svalbard Global Seed Vault on the Norwegian island of Spitsbergen, part of the Svalbard island group.

The seed bank is being built inside a mountain on Spitsbergen Island near the small village of Longyearbyen. It's almost ready for 'business' [as of December 2007] according to their releases. The bank will have dual blast-proof doors with motion sensors, two airlocks, and walls of steel-reinforced concrete one meter thick. It will contain up to three million different varieties of seeds from the entire world, 'so that crop diversity can be conserved for the future,' according to the Norwegian government. Seeds will be specially wrapped to exclude moisture. There will be no full-time staff, but the vault's relative inaccessibility will facilitate monitoring any possible human activity.

Did we miss something here? Their press release stated, 'so that crop diversity can be conserved for the future.' What future do the seed bank's sponsors foresee, that would threaten the global availability of current seeds, almost all of which are already well protected in designated seed banks around the world?

Anytime Bill Gates, the Rockefeller Foundation, Monsanto and Syngenta get together on a common project, it's worth digging a bit deeper behind the rocks on Spitsbergen. When we do we find some fascinating things.

The first notable point is who is sponsoring the doomsday seed vault. Here joining the Norwegians are, as noted, the Bill & Melinda Gates Foundation; the US agribusiness giant DuPont/Pioneer Hi-Bred, one of the world's largest owners of patented genetically-modified (GMO) plant seeds and related agrichemicals; Syngenta, the Swiss-based major GMO seed and agrichemicals company through its Syngenta Foundation; the Rockefeller Foundation, the private group who created the "gene revolution with over $100 million of seed money since the 1970's; CGIAR [Consultative Group on International Agriculture Research], the global network created by the Rockefeller Foundation to promote its ideal of genetic purity through agriculture change. . . ."

CGIAR was shaped at a series of private conferences held at the Rockefeller Foundation's conference center in Bellagio, Italy. Key participants at the Bellagio talks were the Rockefeller Foundation's George Harrar, Ford Foundation's Forrest Hill, Robert McNamara of the World Bank and Maurice Strong, the Rockefeller family's international environmental organizer, who, as a Rockefeller Foundation Trustee, organized the UN

[United Nations] Earth Summit in Stockholm in 1972. It was part of the foundation's decades long focus to turn science to the service of eugenics, a hideous version of racial purity, what has been called The Project.

Genetic Engineering

Now the Svalbard Seed Bank begins to become interesting. But it gets better. 'The Project' I referred to is the project of the Rockefeller Foundation and powerful financial interests since the 1920's to use eugenics, later renamed genetics, to justify creation of a genetically-engineered Master Race. Hitler and the Nazis called it the Ayran Master Race.

The eugenics of Hitler were financed to a major extent by the same Rockefeller Foundation which today is building a doomsday seed vault to preserve samples of every seed on our planet. Now this is getting really intriguing. The same Rockefeller Foundation created the pseudo-science discipline of molecular biology in their relentless pursuit of reducing human life down to the 'defining gene sequence' which, they hoped, could then be modified in order to change human traits at will. Hitler's eugenics scientists, many of whom were quietly brought to the United States after the War to continue their biological eugenics research, laid much of the groundwork of genetic engineering of various life forms, much of it supported openly until well into the Third Reich by Rockefeller Foundation generous grants.

The same Rockefeller Foundation created the so-called Green Revolution,[1] out of a trip to Mexico in 1946 by Nelson Rockefeller and former New Deal Secretary of Agriculture and founder of the Pioneer Hi-Bred Seed Company, Henry Wallace.

The Green Revolution purported to solve the world hunger problem to a major degree in Mexico, India and other se-

---

1. The Green Revolution refers to agricultural advances between the 1940s and 1970s which dramatically increased crop yields.

lect countries where Rockefeller worked. Rockefeller Foundation agronomist, Norman Borlaug, won a Nobel Peace Prize for his work, hardly something to boast about with the likes of [former Secretary of State] Henry Kissinger sharing the same.

In reality, as it years later emerged, the Green Revolution was a brilliant Rockefeller family scheme to develop a globalized agribusiness which they then could monopolize just as they had done in the world oil industry beginning a half century before. As Henry Kissinger declared in the 1970's, 'If you control the oil you control the country; if you control food, you control the population.'

Agribusiness and the Rockefeller Green Revolution went hand-in-hand. They were part of a grand strategy which included Rockefeller Foundation financing of research for the development of genetic engineering of plants and animals a few years later.

John H. Davis had been Assistant Agriculture Secretary under President Dwight Eisenhower in the early 1950's. He left Washington in 1955 and went to the Harvard Graduate School of Business, an unusual place for an agriculture expert in those days. He had a clear strategy. In 1956, Davis wrote an article in the *Harvard Business Review* in which he declared that "the only way to solve the so-called farm problem once and for all, and avoid cumbersome government programs, is to progress from agriculture to agribusiness." He knew precisely what he had in mind, though few others had a clue back then—a revolution in agriculture production that would concentrate control of the food chain in corporate multinational hands, away from the traditional family farmer.

A crucial aspect driving the interest of the Rockefeller Foundation and US agribusiness companies was the fact that the Green Revolution was based on proliferation of new hybrid seeds in developing markets. One vital aspect of hybrid seeds was their lack of reproductive capacity. Hybrids had a built in protection against multiplication. Unlike normal open pollinated species whose seed gave yields similar to its parents, the yield of the seed borne by hybrid plants was significantly lower than that of the first generation.

That declining yield characteristic of hybrids meant farmers must normally buy seed every year in order to obtain high yields. Moreover, the lower yield of the second generation eliminated the trade in seed that was often done by seed producers without the breeder's authorization. It prevented the redistribution of the commercial crop seed by middlemen. If the large multinational seed companies were able to control the parental seed lines in house, no competitor or farmer would be able to produce the hybrid. The global concentration of hybrid seed patents into a handful of giant seed companies, led by DuPont's Pioneer Hi-Bred and Monsanto's Dekalb laid the ground for the later GMO seed revolution.

Enforced Dependency

In effect, the introduction of modern American agricultural technology, chemical fertilizers and commercial hybrid seeds all made local farmers in developing countries, particularly the larger more established ones, dependent on foreign, mostly US agribusiness and petro-chemical company inputs. It was a first step in what was to be a decades-long, carefully planned process.

Under the Green Revolution, Agribusiness was making major inroads into markets which were previously of limited access to US exporters. The trend was later dubbed "market-oriented agriculture." In reality it was agribusiness-controlled agriculture.

Through the Green Revolution, the Rockefeller Foundation and later Ford Foundation worked hand-in-hand shaping and supporting the foreign policy goals of the United States Agency for International Development (USAID) and of the CIA [Central Intelligence Agency].

One major effect of the Green Revolution was to depopulate the countryside of peasants who were forced to flee into shantytown slums around the cities in desperate search for work. That was no accident; it was part of the plan to create cheap labor pools for forthcoming US multinational manufactures, the 'globalization' of recent years.

When the self-promotion around the Green Revolution died down, the results were quite different from what had been promised. Problems had arisen from indiscriminate use of the new chemical pesticides, often with serious health consequences. The mono-culture cultivation of new hybrid seed varieties decreased soil fertility and yields over time. The first results were impressive: double or even triple yields for some crops such as wheat and later corn in Mexico. That soon faded.

The Green Revolution was typically accompanied by large irrigation projects which often included World Bank loans to construct huge new dams, and flood[ed] previously settled areas and fertile farmland in the process. Also, super-wheat produced greater yields by saturating the soil with huge amounts of fertilizer per acre, the fertilizer being the product of nitrates and petroleum, commodities controlled by the Rockefeller-dominated Seven Sisters major oil companies.

Huge quantities of herbicides and pesticides were also used, creating additional markets for the oil and chemical giants. As one analyst put it, in effect, the Green Revolution was merely a chemical revolution. At no point could developing nations pay for the huge amounts of chemical fertilizers and pesticides. They would get the credit courtesy of the World Bank and special loans by Chase Bank and other large New York banks, backed by US Government guarantees.

Applied in a large number of developing countries, those loans went mostly to the large landowners. For the smaller peasants the situation worked differently. Small peasant farmers could not afford the chemical and other modern inputs and had to borrow money.

Initially various government programs tried to provide some loans to farmers so that they could purchase seeds and fertilizers. Farmers who could not participate in this kind of program had to borrow from the private sector. Because of the exorbitant interest rates for informal loans, many small farmers did not even get the benefits of the initial higher yields. After harvest, they had to sell most if not all of their produce to pay off loans and interest. They became dependent on money-lenders and traders and often lost their land. Even with soft loans from government agencies, growing subsistence crops gave way to the production of cash crops.

Since decades, the same interests including the Rockefeller Foundation which backed the initial Green Revolution, have worked to promote a second 'Gene Revolution' as Rockefeller Foundation President Gordon Conway termed it several years ago, the spread of industrial agriculture and commercial inputs including GMO patented seeds.

Gates, Rockefeller and a Green Revolution in Africa

With the true background of the 1950's Rockefeller Foundation Green Revolution clear in mind, it becomes especially curious that the same Rockefeller Foundation along with the Gates Foundation, which are now investing millions of dollars in preserving every seed against a possible "doomsday" scenario, are also investing millions in a project called The Alliance for a Green Revolution [AGRA] in Africa.

AGRA, as it calls itself, is an alliance again with the same Rockefeller Foundation which created the "Gene Revolution." A look at the AGRA Board of Directors confirms this....

While to date they are keeping a low profile, Monsanto and the major GMO agribusiness giants are believed [to be] at the heart of using ... AGRA to spread their patented GMO seeds across Africa under the deceptive label, 'bio-technology,' the new euphemism for genetically engineered patented seeds. To date South Africa is the only African country permitting legal planting of GMO crops. In 2003 Burkina Faso authorized GMO trials. In 2005 ... Ghana drafted bio-safety legislation and key officials expressed their intentions to pursue research into GMO crops.

Africa is the next target in the US-government campaign to spread GMO worldwide. Its rich soils make it an ideal candidate. Not surprisingly many African governments suspect the worst from the GMO sponsors as a multitude of genetic engineering and biosafety projects have been initiated in Africa, with the aim of introducing GMOs into Africa's agricultural systems. These include sponsorships offered by the US government to train African scientists in genetic engineering in the US, biosafety projects funded by the United States Agency for International Development (USAID) and the World Bank; GMO research involving African indigenous food crops. . . .

The Purpose of Svalbard

What leads the Gates and Rockefeller foundations to at one and the same time to back proliferation of patented ... seeds across Africa, a process which, as it has in every other place on earth, destroys the plant seed varieties as monoculture industrialized agribusiness is introduced? At the same time they invest tens of millions of dollars to preserve every seed variety known in a bomb-proof doomsday vault near the remote Arctic Circle 'so that crop diversity can be conserved for the future' to restate their official release? . . .

We can legitimately ask why Bill Gates and the Rockefeller Foundation along with the major genetic engineering agribusiness giants such as DuPont and Syngenta, along with CGIAR are building the Doomsday Seed Vault in the Arctic.

Who uses such a seed bank in the first place? Plant breeders and researchers are the major users of gene banks. Today's largest plant breeders are Monsanto, DuPont, Syngenta and Dow Chemical, the global plant-patenting GMO giants. Since early in 2007 Monsanto holds world patent rights together with the United States Government for plant so-called 'Terminator' or Genetic Use Restriction Technology (GURT). Terminator is an ominous technology by which a patented commercial seed commits 'suicide' after one harvest. Control by private seed companies is total. Such control and power over the food chain has never before in the history of mankind existed.

This clever genetically engineered terminator trait forces farmers to return every year to Monsanto or other GMO seed suppliers to get new seeds for rice, soybeans, corn, wheat, whatever major crops they need to feed their population. If broadly introduced around the world, it could within perhaps a decade or so make the world's majority of food producers new feudal serfs in bondage to three or four giant seed companies such as Monsanto or DuPont or Dow Chemical.

That, of course, could also open the door to have those private companies, perhaps under orders from their host government, Washington [D.C.], deny seeds to one or another developing country whose politics happened to go against Washington's. Those who say 'It can't happen here' should look more closely at current global events. The mere existence of that concentration of power in three or four private US-based agribusiness giants is grounds for legally banning all GMO crops even were their harvest gains real, which they manifestly are not. . . .

Biowarfare and Extinction

Now we come to the heart of the danger and the potential for misuse inherent in the Svalbard project of Bill Gates and the Rockefeller Foundation. Can the development of patented seeds for most of the world's major sustenance crops such as rice, corn, wheat, and feed grains such as soybeans ultimately be used in a horrible form of biological warfare?

The explicit aim of the eugenics lobby funded by wealthy elite families such as Rockefeller, Carnegie, Harriman and others since the 1920's, has embodied what they termed 'negative eugenics,' the systematic killing off of undesired bloodlines. Margaret Sanger, a . . . eugenicist, the founder of Planned Parenthood International and an intimate of the Rockefeller family, created something called The Negro Project in 1939, based in Harlem, which as she confided in a letter to a friend, was all about the fact that, as she put it, 'we want to exterminate the Negro population.'

A small California biotech company, Epicyte, in 2001 announced the development of genetically engineered corn which contained a spermicide which made the semen of men who ate it sterile. At the time Epicyte had a joint venture agreement to spread its technology with DuPont and Syngenta, two of the sponsors of the Svalbard Doomsday Seed Vault. Epicyte was since acquired by a North Carolina biotech company. Astonishing to learn was that Epicyte had developed its spermicidal GMO corn with research funds from the US Department of Agriculture, the same USDA which, despite worldwide opposition, continued to finance the development of Terminator technology, now held by Monsanto.

In the 1990's the UN's World Health Organization [WHO] launched a campaign to vaccinate millions of women in Nicaragua, Mexico and the Philippines between the ages of 15 and 45, allegedly against Tentanus, a sickness arising from such things as stepping on a rusty nail. The vaccine was not given to men or boys, despite the fact they are presumably equally liable to step on rusty nails as women.

Because of that curious anomaly, Comite Pro Vida de Mexico, a Roman Catholic lay organization became suspicious and had vaccine samples tested. The tests revealed that the

Tetanus vaccine being spread by the WHO only to women of child-bearing age contained human Chorionic Gonadotrophin or hCG, a natural hormone which when combined with a tetanus toxoid carrier stimulated antibodies rendering a woman incapable of maintaining a pregnancy. None of the women vaccinated were told.

It later came out that the Rockefeller Foundation along with the Rockefeller's Population Council, the World Bank (home to CGIAR), and the United States' National Institutes of Health had been involved in a 20-year-long project begun in 1972 to develop the concealed abortion vaccine with a tetanus carrier for WHO. In addition, the Government of Norway, the host to the Svalbard Doomsday Seed Vault, donated $41 million to develop the special abortive Tetanus vaccine.

Is it a coincidence that these same organizations, from Norway to the Rockefeller Foundation to the World Bank are also involved in the Svalbard seed bank project? According to Prof. Francis Boyle who drafted the Biological Weapons Anti-Terrorism Act of 1989 enacted by the US Congress, the Pentagon is 'now gearing up to fight and win biological warfare' as part of two [George W.] Bush national strategy directives adopted, he notes, 'without public knowledge and review' in 2002. Boyle adds that in 2001–2004 alone the US Federal Government spent $14.5 billion for civilian bio-warfare-related work, a staggering sum.

Rutgers University biologist Richard Ebright estimates that over 300 scientific institutions and some 12,000 individuals in the USA today have access to pathogens suitable for biowarfare. Alone there are 497 US Government NIH [National Institutes of Health] grants for research into infectious diseases with biowarfare potential. Of course this is being justified under the rubric of defending against a possible terror attack as so much is today.

Many of the US Government dollars spent on biowarfare research involve genetic engineering. MIT [Massachusetts Institute of Technology] biology professor Jonathan King says that the 'growing bio-terror programs represent a significant emerging danger to our own population.' King adds, 'while such programs are always called defensive, with biological weapons, defensive and offensive programs overlap almost completely.'

Time will tell whether, God Forbid, the Svalbard Dooms-day Seed Bank of Bill Gates and the Rockefeller Foundation is part of another Final Solution, this involving the extinction of the Late, Great Planet Earth.

> *"The mysterious nature of materials manufactured at the nanoscale—just a few atoms thick, or 10,000 times thinner than a human hair—has led some to fear the technology's toxic power."*

Scientists Should Prepare for Nanotechnology Disaster Scenarios

Dave Levitan

Dave Levitan is a journalist who writes about environmental issues, health, and medicine. In the following viewpoint, he reports that researchers are investigating the possible toxic effects of nanotechnology. Nanotechnology refers to materials manufactured at an extremely small scale. Because little is known about these materials, there is a concern that they may have dangerous environmental or biological effects. Even though apocalyptic scenarios involving nanotechnology are unlikely, Levitan says, it is still important to begin testing early to avoid any possible negative consequences.

Dave Levitan, "Keeping the Grey Goo at Bay," Scienceline, December 19, 2008. Copyright © 2010 NYU Journalism. Reproduced by permission.

As you read, consider the following questions:

1. According to Levitan, what doomsday scenario did nanotechnology pioneer K. Eric Drexler discuss and later regret discussing?

2. According to André Nel, how many of the 50,000 man-made chemicals have been tested for toxicity?

3. What are mesocosms, according to Levitan?

Everyone's favorite environmental villain, DDT, was first synthesized in 1874 and then put into widespread use as an insecticide following World War II. After Rachel Carson's 1962 exposé *Silent Spring* pushed the government to seriously investigate the chemical's effects, DDT was finally banned in the United States in 1972, almost a century after its creation.

Grey Goo

Thanks largely to this cautionary tale, researchers in emerging fields like nanotechnology now actively attempt to ferret out potential hazards before they occur. The mysterious nature of materials manufactured at the nanoscale—just a few atoms thick, or 10,000 times thinner than a human hair—has led some to fear the technology's toxic power. Famously, early nanotechnology pioneer K. Eric Drexler discussed—and later regretted discussing—the frightening potential for self-assembling nanosized robots to turn all living matter into lifeless "grey goo."

While the grey goo scenario is certainly unlikely, little is known about the effects nanoparticles may have on the environment and human health. To fill that knowledge gap, a recent $38 million grant from the National Science Foundation and the Environmental Protection Agency established two Centers for the Environmental Implications of Nanotechnology, or CEINs, at Duke University and the University of California, Los Angeles [UCLA].

"There are probably 500 to 600 different engineered nano-materials that are already in some product," said André Nel, director of the UCLA CEIN. "But imagine that in 20 years we may have 600,000." The technology can already be found in products like stain-resistant pants and sunscreen, but most experts agree with Nel that this industry is on the brink of a manufacturing explosion. The National Science Foundation projects that nanotechnology will be a $1 trillion industry by 2015, with countless applications ranging from cosmetics to computer chips to cancer treatments.

Nel contrasted the early start of this nanotechnology testing process with that of the chemical industry from which the DDT catastrophe sprang: of the 50,000 man-made chemicals fewer, than 1,000 have been tested for toxicity. "We are fortunate to start with a relatively clean slate," he said. "We do not know of a single human disease or a single environmental or ecological disaster that has been caused by an engineered nanomaterial."

But Cal Baier-Anderson, a toxicologist with the Environmental Defense Fund in Washington, D.C., said some studies have hinted at negative effects on fish or bacteria with certain nanomaterials. She explained that the strange properties many nanomaterials exhibit—from increased strength to changes in thermal and magnetic characteristics—make understanding their environmental effects difficult. "It adds a vast layer of complexity to . . . how differences in the engineering, processing or manufacture of these materials can impact [their] transport in the environment and toxicological hazards," she said.

Investigating Potential Harm

The UCLA CEIN will employ a predictive computer modeling technique aimed at finding types of nanoparticles that may cause harm to ecosystems or biological organisms. At Duke,

The Danger of Grey Goo

When nanotechnology-based manufacturing was first proposed, a concern arose that tiny manufacturing systems might run amok and 'eat' the biosphere, reducing it to copies of themselves. In 1986, [nanotechnology pioneer K.] Eric Drexler wrote, "We cannot afford certain kinds of accidents with replicating assemblers."

Grey goo would entail five capabilities integrated into one small package. These capabilities are: Mobility—the ability to travel through the environment; Shell—a thin but effective barrier to keep out diverse chemicals and ultraviolet light; Control—a complete set of blueprints and the computers to interpret them (even working at the nanoscale, this will take significant space); Metabolism—breaking down random chemicals into simple feedstock; and Fabrication—turning feedstock into nanosystems.

Although grey goo has essentially no military and no commercial value, and only limited terrorist value, it could be used as a tool for blackmail.

Development and use of molecular manufacturing poses absolutely no risk of creating grey goo by accident at any point. However, goo type systems do not appear to be ruled out by the laws of physics, and we cannot ignore the possibility that the five stated requirements could be combined deliberately at some point, in a device smart enough that cleanup would be costly and difficult.

Center for Responsible Nanotechnology (CRN),
"Dangers of Molecular Manufacturing," www.crnano.org.

researchers will use small, controlled environments known as mesocosms in order to test the effects of various nanomaterials.

The mesocosms, which are in essence large terrariums, will allow researchers to release nanomaterials into complex systems that cannot otherwise be simulated. "The impacts of nanomaterials on an individual organism may be different in a mesocosm sphere than it would be in a laboratory," said Mark Wiesner, director of the Duke CEIN. He added that the mesocosms, which are currently being constructed in Duke Forest, can be adapted to mimic a variety of ecosystems. The first one tested over the course of the next year will be a wetland.

It is in humanity's best interest to avoid another disastrous *Silent Spring* scenario, but technology historian and author Edward Tenner points out that overreactions are commonplace when a paradigm-shifting technology emerges.

"There is a long history of technology that has had messianic hopes but has turned out to be much more limited and prosaic," Tenner said. He added that the major risks of new technologies often appear in areas far removed from those initially imagined, making effective predictive testing extremely difficult. "Most of reality is in that messy intermediate zone, as opposed to electronic levitation and grey goo."

Even with the difficulties involved in risk prediction, Nel said starting the environmental testing process now is crucial. "We're at the beginning of a revolution," he said. "If you wait until you see injury and then clean up, you're going to be very much behind the curve. We need the knowledge now."

> *"A true AI [artificial intelligence] would have immense economic potential, and when money is at stake, safety issues get put aside until real problems develop—at which time, of course, it may already be too late."*

Artificial Intelligence Poses a Doomsday Threat

Kaj Sotala

Kaj Sotala is a writer and a supporter of the Singularity Institute. In the following viewpoint, he argues that an artificial intelligence (AI) will not be dedicated to destroying humans, as depicted in film. However, Sotala says, the AI will not care about humans either. Thus, it may attack or eliminate humans as a byproduct of other goals or interests. Sotala says that the threat from AI means that scientists working on artificial intelligence must be careful to develop ways to make AI care about human beings.

As you read, consider the following questions:

1. Why does Sotala argue that the *Terminator* movie may lead people to believe that AI is not dangerous?

Kaj Sotala, "Thinking of AIs as Humans Is Misguided," PreventingSkynet.com, May 27, 2009. Reproduced by permission of the author.

2. According to Sotala, what is inductive bias?

3. What does Stephen Omohundro conclude about agents with harmless goals?

Skynet in the *Terminator*[1] movies is a powerful, evocative warning of the destructive force an artificial intelligence [AI] could potentially wield. However, as counterintuitive as it may sound, I find that the *Terminator* franchise is actually making many people *underestimate* the danger posed by AI.

AI Is Not Human

It goes like this. A person watches a *Terminator* movie and sees Skynet portrayed as a force actively dedicated to the destruction of humanity. Later on the same person hears somebody bring up the dangers of AI. He then recalls the *Terminator* movies and concludes (correctly so!) that a vision of an artificial intelligence spontaneously deciding to exterminate all of humanity is unrealistic. Seeing the other person's claims as unrealistic and inspired by silly science fiction, he dismisses the AI threat argument as hopelessly misguided.

Yet humans are not actively seeking to harm animals when they level a forest in order to build luxury housing where the forest once stood. The animals living in the forest are harmed regardless, not out of an act of intentional malice, but as a simple side-effect. [AI researcher] Eliezer Yudkowsky put it well: *the AI does not hate you, nor does it love you, but you are made out of atoms which it can use for something else.*

To assume an artificial intelligence would necessarily act in a way we wanted is just as misguided and anthropomorphic as assuming that it would automatically be hostile and seek to rebel out of a desire for freedom. Usually, a child will love its parents and caretakers, and protégés will care for their patrons—but these are traits that have developed in us over

1. *Terminator* is a 1984 science fiction movie in which an artificial intelligence known as Skynet takes over the world.

countless generations of evolutionary change, not givens for any intelligent mind. An AI built from scratch would have no reason to care about its creators, unless it was expressly designed to do so. And even if it was, a designer building the AI to care about her must very closely consider what she actually *means* by "caring"—for these things are not givens, even if we think of them as self-contained concepts obvious to any intelligent mind. It only seems so because we instinctively model other minds by using ourselves and people we know as templates—to do otherwise would mean freezing up, as we'd spend years building from scratch models of every new person we met. The people we know and consider intelligent all have at least roughly the same idea of what "caring" for someone means, thus any AI would eventually arrive at the same concept, right?

An *inductive bias* is a tendency to learn certain kinds of rules from certain kinds of observations. Occam's razor, the principle of choosing the simplest consistent hypothesis, is one kind of inductive bias. So is an infant's tendency to eventually start ignoring phoneme differences [the basic units of speech sounds] not relevant for their native language. Inductive biases are necessary for learning, for without them, there would be an infinite number of explanations for any phenomena—but nothing says that all intelligent minds should have the same inductive biases as inbuilt. Caring for someone is such a complex concept that it couldn't be built into the AI directly—the designer would have to come up with inductive biases she thought would eventually lead to the mind learning to care about us, in a fashion we'd interpret as caring.

AI Will Not Care About Us

The evolutionary psychologists John Tooby and Leda Cosmides write: *Evolution tailors computational hacks that work brilliantly, by exploiting relationships that exist only in its particular fragment of the universe (the geometry of parallax gives vision a*

Robots Designed with Harmless Goals May Behave in Harmful Ways

Surely no harm could come from building a chess-playing robot, could it? We argue that such a robot will indeed be dangerous unless it is designed very carefully. Without special precautions, it will resist being turned off, will try to break into other machines and make copies of itself, and will try to acquire resources without regard for anyone else's safety. These potentially harmful behaviors will occur not because they were programmed in at the start, but because of the intrinsic nature of goal driven systems.

Stephen M. Omohundro, "The Basic AI Drives,"
Self-Aware Systems, January 25, 2008.

depth cue: an infant nursed by your mother is your genetic sibling: two solid objects cannot occupy the same space). These native intelligences are dramatically smarter than general reasoning because natural selection equipped them with radical short cuts. Our minds have evolved to reason about other human minds, not minds-in-general. When trying to predict how an AI would behave in a certain situation, and thus trying to predict how to make it safe, we cannot help but unconsciously slip in assumptions based on how humans would behave. The inductive biases we automatically employ to predict human behavior do not correctly predict AI behavior. Because we are not used to questioning deep-rooted assumptions of such hypotheses, we easily fail to do so even in the case of AI, where it would actually be necessary.

The people who *have* stopped to question those assumptions have arrived at unsettling results. In his "Basic AI Drives" paper, Stephen Omohundro concludes that even agents with seemingly harmless goals will, if intelligent enough, have a strong tendency to try to achieve those goals via less harmless methods. As simple examples, any AI with a desire to achieve any kinds of goals will have a motivation to resist being turned off, as that would prevent it from achieving the goal; and because of this, it will have a motivation to acquire resources it can use to protect itself. While this won't make it desire humanity's destruction, it is not inconceivable that it would be motivated to at least reduce humanity to a state where we couldn't even potentially pose a threat.

A commonly-heard objection to these kinds of scenarios is that the scientists working on AI will surely be aware of these risks themselves, and be careful enough. But historical precedent doesn't really support this assumption. Even if the scientists themselves were careful, they will often be under intense pressure, especially when economic interest is at stake. Climate scientists have spent decades warning people of the threat posed by greenhouse gasses, but even today many nations are reluctant to cut back on emissions, as they suspect it'd disadvantage them economically. The engineers in charge of building many Soviet nuclear plants, most famously Chernobyl, did not put safety as their first priority, and so on. A true AI would have immense economic potential, and when money is at stake, safety issues get put aside until real problems develop—at which time, of course, it may already be too late.

Yet if we want to avoid Skynet-like scenarios, we cannot afford to risk it. Safety must be a paramount priority in the creation of Artificial Intelligence.

> *"Despite what* Wired *may think, mankind will never face a technological singularity. Why? Computers are dumb assholes."*

Neither AI nor Nanotech Poses a Doomsday Threat

Zack Parsons

Zack Parsons is an editor at Something Awful. *In the following viewpoint, he argues that the great advances promised for nanotechnology and artificial intelligence (AI) have not occurred, and that doomsday scenarios involving these technologies are therefore very unlikely. He says that AI robots cannot perform simple tasks and that nanotechnology has managed to accomplish little if anything. He concludes that the singularity—the point at which technology will become so advanced that mankind will be irrelevant—will never occur.*

As you read, consider the following questions:

1. How does Parsons explain Moore's Law?

2. What breakthroughs were promised in nanotechnology in the article Parsons said he read in sixth or seventh grade?

Zack Parsons, "The Lie of the Technological Singularity," Somethingawful.com, September 28, 2007. Reproduced by permission.

3. Parsons says that the technological singularity is about as believable as what?

E verybody has a doomsday.

Christians have their baroque delusions about the Rapture [some Christian fundamentalists believe that Christians will be gathered in the air to meet Jesus at his return]. Liberals have global warming scenarios where Manhattan [New York] ends up looking like something out of anime. Conservatives fixate on immigrants flooding our borders until we're all speaking their devil tongue and voting for brown presidents.

The Singularity

For the 100 million atheist thyroid cases that live on the Internet day and night there is the concept of the technological singularity. The idea is that at some point in the future, technology will become so advanced that mankind will be irrelevant. It's a cross between your usual end-of-all-things doomsday scenario and an orgasmic apotheosis wherein the Asperger's sufferers get to leave behind their troublesome flesh and be downloaded into a greeting card microchip.

[Online magazine] *Wired* tends to write an article about the approaching technological singularity whenever it's a slow month in [the virtual world] Second Life. Their theories range from super-intelligent AIs [artificial intelligences] taking over the world and exterminating mankind, to cybernetic upgrades creating super humans, to all-consuming swarms of nano-machines that devour and multiply until there is nothing left alive on earth.

One of the concepts frequently referenced in technological singularity theories is that of "Moore's Law." To grossly simplify Moore's Law it is the rule that every two years, thanks to technological improvement, the processing power of a computer doubles. Eventually it doubles enough and computers get fast enough that the world ends or we're in the Matrix or something.

I find it difficult to believe anyone could reach this sort of conclusion logically. If someone told me race cars doubled in speed every two years my conclusion would not be, "Eventually they will kill us all!"

Despite what *Wired* may think, mankind will never face a technological singularity. Why? Computers are dumb assholes.

Computers Are Not a Real Threat

Exhibit A: The Internet Makes You Stupid. Ah, the Internet, centerpiece of the information age, the interactive ideascape where great minds come together to create a collective consciousness. Surely the Internet represents the most likely vector for the coming technological singularity.

Wait a second. Do any of the people talking about a technological singularity actually use the Internet? It's a maelstrom of idiocy and moral decay. The triumphs of the Internet like YouTube and Wikipedia? They are shining examples that when a lot of people put their heads together the result is Chocolate Rain and its corresponding 1,200-word Wikipedia article.

If the collective mind of the Internet somehow becomes self-aware it's probably going to spend the next 10,000 years perfecting its Prince of Tennis wiki site. Like the gelatinous human minds that gave birth to it, Internet 3.0 will have zero interest in doing anything productive or destructive, thus proving the old math theory that zero multiplied by any number still equals a collection of genetic rejects, sexual deviants, and sociopaths obsessed with minutiae.

Exhibit B: 21st Century AI Is 5,000 Zombie Computers Sending ... Spam for the Ukrainian Mob. This one is pretty self explanatory, but of the two most powerful computing systems in the world one is devoted to trying to find spam aliens and the other is owned by the Ukrainian mob to send spare emails for unscrupulous clients. Even the military and intelligence super-networks are just Google Earth with a crosshair and maybe [fictional character] Jason Bourne's bio in a tabbed window. Modern processing power is distributed and used for really stupid crap that will never result in Skynet [the evil artificial intelligence in the *Terminator* movies] launching nukes.

Nanotechnology

Exhibit C: Useful Nanotechnology Is Approximately 1 Billion Years Away. I remember reading an article in sixth or seventh grade about how a secret government lab inside a tree trunk in some black ops forest in California was nearing a breakthrough with nanotechnology. Within a year or two they would be producing "the first of many" tiny robots smaller than a grain of sand that people could inject into their blood stream to clear clogged arteries. What has nanotechnology yielded in the more than 15 years since I read that article?

We have carbon nanotubes, which we get to pretend is nanotechnology because pretty much everything else about nanotechnology, including everything interesting, was bullshit. Now your bicycle seat weighs one ounce less and can stop a knife or something. Progress!

Oh, and they put glasses on a f---ing fly. I can practically feel that grey goo[1] gnawing away at my marrow!

Exhibit D: My Dumbass TiVo. My TiVo [a digital video recorder] continually records movies I would never watch on channels I do not even have. I'll turn on the TV and find my TiVo recording the ninth rerun of the *Colbert Report* even though I told it to record only first run episodes. When I try to change the channel the TiVo will pop up a message and

1. Grey goo was an apocalyptic scenario in which self-replicating nanomachines were supposed to turn all matter into goo.

warn me the other tuner is recording something, so I go into the menu and discover the stupid thing is recording a *Very Brady Sequel* on "Starz!"

Then the next day I realize that the TiVo was doing all of this while it was supposed to be recording something I specifically told it to record. Like an infuriating *Frontline* episode detailing what [former Vice President] Dick Cheney did to democracy with the help of one of those oily cretins that orbit him like satellites made out of law degrees. Law degrees from a law school with "Bible" in the name where they teach you that cutting molars out of Muslims is not only constitutional, but actually honors Christ.

Singularity my ass, figure that shit out TiVo!

Exhibit E: Those Stupid Asimo Robots Can't Do Shit. Every six months the Internet buzzes with excitement over some chirpy hunk of plastic shit from Japan that looks like a midget astronaut. YouTube videos are posted to forums far and wide . . .

Meanwhile, the robots in the video are usually ambling around at the speed of a polio cripple, holding a trumpet up to their astronaut helmet, or failing to descend a staircase successfully. Nine times out of ten my 96 year old grandma can pull that incredible feat off and this is a woman that thinks gay people are a kind of Chinese.

We're not exactly closing in on the rise of the machines with these Japanese robots. They're walking Furbies [a popular electronics toy] with inner-ear disorders. . . .

Biotech? Space elevators? I don't think so.

Unless the world can end by downloading the wrong ringtone from a company advertising on MTV2 I'm afraid the technological singularity is about as believable as a lamb figuring out how to open vials.

Hmm, maybe the lamb and Asimo[2] can work together to figure it out.

---

2. ASIMO is a humanoid robot made by Honda.

Periodical and Internet Sources Bibliography

The following articles have been selected to supplement the diverse views presented in this chapter.

Ronald Bailey	"Wagging the 'Fat Tail' of Climate Catastrophe," Reason.com, February 10, 2009. http://reason.com.
Jeanna Bryner	"'Doomsday' Seed Vault Stores 500,000 Crops," LiveScience.com, March 10, 2010. www.livescience.com.
Michel Chossudovsky	"Real Versus Fake Crises: Concealing the Risk of an All Out Nuclear War," GlobalResearch.ca, September 16, 2010. http://globalresearch.ca.
Stephen J. Dubner	"A Different Climate Change Apocalypse Than the One You Were Envisioning," *Freakonomics*, July 7, 2008. http://freakonomics.blogs.nytimes.com.
Robert Lamb	"Noel Sharkey: Robotics vs. Sci-Fi vs. Anthropomorphism," *HowStuffWorks*, May 25, 2010. http://blogs.howstuffworks.com.
Cole Morton	"The Large Hadron Collider: End of the World, or God's Own Spin?" *Independent*, September 7, 2008. www.independent.co.uk.
John Mueller	"Why Nuclear Weapons Aren't as Frightening as You Think," *Foreign Policy*, January/February 2010. www.foreignpolicy.com.
Dennis Overbye	"Gauging a Collider's Odds of Creating a Black Hole," *New York Times*, April 15, 2008. www.nytimes.com.
Eliezer Yudkowsky	"Why We Need Friendly AI," *Terminator Salvation: Preventing Skynet*, May 22, 2009. www.preventingskynet.com.

For Further Discussion

Chapter 1

1. B.A. Robinson notes that Y2K caused some computer failures, but nothing apocalyptic. Does this contradict the article by Catherine Winter, or can the two viewpoints be reconciled—and if so, how?

2. In Brandon Keim's viewpoint, interviewee Lawrence Joseph suggests that the United States should prepare for 2012 just in case there is a disaster. Would Craig Smith agree? What downsides might there be to preparing for a disaster that did not occur?

Chapter 2

1. The leader of the Ghost Dance movement discussed in the viewpoint by William Kornblum was named Jack Wilson, or Wovoka. How might Peter A. Olsson's theories be applied to Wilson's Ghost Dance movement? Do you think using Olsson's psychological theories for the Ghost Dance movement is useful, or does Kornblum's sociological approach seem more appropriate?

2. Bill Barnwell argues that a belief in the rapture can lead Christians to criticize those who try to change the world for the better. Does Paul Proctor criticize those who try to change the world? How would Proctor respond to James P. Pinkerton and his use of Christianity?

Chapter 3

1. Tad Daley notes that the Barack Obama administration still maintains the policy option for America to start a nuclear war. Does Gerard DeGroot suggest that such a policy increases the likelihood of nuclear war? Based on

DeGroot's article, would threatening North Korea or Iran with a nuclear first strike be a useful policy? Why or why not?

2. Does Kevin Shapiro argue that there is no real danger of a global warming catastrophe, or does he argue that such a catastrophe, even if imminent, can not be prevented at this point? Or does he say both? Does it make sense to ignore problems if there are no good solutions to them?

3. Does F. William Engdahl provide any direct evidence for his assertion that Bill Gates and other investors are using the Svalbard Global Seed Vault for dangerous biowarfare research? What evidence does he provide, and how convincing is this evidence?

4. Zack Parsons' viewpoint is a humor piece rather than a serious argument. Does he successfully refute or call into question any of the points made by Dave Levitan or Kaj Sotala? How does his use of humor impact his argument?

Organizations to Contact

The editors have compiled the following list of organizations concerned with the issues debated in this book. The descriptions are derived from materials provided by the organizations. All have publications or information available for interested readers. The list was compiled on the date of publication of the present volume; the information provided here may change. Be aware that many organizations take several weeks or longer to respond to inquiries, so allow as much time as possible.

The American Civil Defense Association (TACDA)
11576 S State St., Suite #502, Draper, UT 84020
(800) 425-5397 • fax: (888) 425-5339
e-mail: defense@tacda.org
website: www.tacda.org

TACDA was established in the early 1960s in an effort to help promote civil defense awareness and disaster preparedness, both in the military and private sector, and to assist citizens in their efforts to prepare for all types of natural and man-made disasters. Publications include the quarterly *Journal of Civil Defense*.

Arms Control Association (ACA)
1313 L St. NW, Suite 130, Washington, DC 20005
(202) 463-8270 • fax: (202) 463-8273
e-mail: aca@armscontrol.org
website: www.armscontrol.org

The Arms Control Association is a nonprofit organization dedicated to promoting public understanding of and support for effective arms control policies. ACA seeks to increase public appreciation of the need to limit arms, reduce international tensions, and promote world peace. It publishes the monthly magazine *Arms Control Today*, articles from which are available on its website. Its website also includes news, threat assessment briefs, reports, book reviews, interviews, and other resources.

Cato Institute

1000 Massachusetts Ave. NW, Washington, DC   20001-5403
(202) 842-0200 • fax: (202) 842-3490
website: www.cato.org

The Cato Institute is an organization dedicated to espousing the libertarian principles of free market economics and limited government intervention in all areas of life. As such, Cato promotes energy and environmental policy that discourages government policies and incentives to push the development of sustainable energy sources, instead advocating for the free market's ability to provide the best solutions to environmental issues such as global warming. The institute worries that government intervention to protect the environment will only stifle economic liberty. Current articles and studies by Cato concerning global warming include, "What to Do About Climate Change," "Is the Sky Really Falling? A Review of Recent Global Warming Scare Stories," and "Shaky Science: Inconvenient Truths Ignored by EPA in Its Proposal to Regulate Carbon Dioxide Emissions." These and others are available online.

CERN: European Organization for Nuclear Research

CERN CH-1211, Genéve 23
   Switzerland
+41 22 76 761 111 • fax: +41 22 76 765 55
e-mail: press.office@cern.ch
website: http://public.web.cern.ch/public/

CERN, a European joint venture, is one of the world's largest centers for scientific research. It is dedicated to the study of fundamental physics, especially through the use of particle accelerators and detectors. Its website includes extensive information on CERN's mission, basic science, particle accelerators, ongoing experiments, and more.

Cult Hotline & Clinic (CHC)

135 W 50th St., 6th Floor, New York, NY   10020
(212) 632-4640
e-mail: info@cultclinic.org
website: www.cultclinic.org

The Cult Hotline & Clinic was founded in 1980 to serve families and friends of cult members, former cult members, and to educate community groups most at risk of interaction with cults. CHC is a nonprofit, non-sectarian counseling and education organization working with people of all religious, ethnic, and racial backgrounds. The organization offers a hotline and counseling services for parents of cult followers, who are often worried, upset, and confused about what to do; former cult members, who often suffer from persistent psychological aftereffects and need intensive clinical treatment; and susceptible community members, who may be approached by people using misleading recruitment techniques. Articles and testimonials from former cult members are available on the website.

International Cultic Studies Association (ICSA)

PO Box 2265, Bonita Springs, FL   34133
(239) 514-3081 • fax: (305) 393-8193
e-mail: mail@icsamail.com
website: www.icsahome.com

Founded in 1979, the International Cultic Studies Association is a global network of people concerned about psychological manipulation and abuse in cultic groups, alternative movements, and other environments. In order to help affected families and individuals, enhance the skills of helping professionals, and forewarn those who might become involved in harmful group situations, ICSA collects and disseminates information through periodicals and websites, conducts and encourages research, maintains an information phone line, and runs workshops and conferences. ICSA consists of and responds to the needs of people interested in cults, new religious movements, sects, and spiritual abuse. Publications include *ICSA Today* and *Cultic Studies Review*.

Lifeboat Foundation
1638 Esmeralda Ave., Minden, NV   89423
(775) 783-8443 • fax: (775) 783-0803
e-mail: education@lifeboat.com
website: www.lifeboat.com

The Lifeboat Foundation is a nonprofit nongovernmental organization dedicated to encouraging scientific advancements while helping humanity survive existential risks and possible misuse of increasingly powerful technologies, including genetic engineering, nanotechnology, and robotics/artificial intelligence (AI). Its website contains a number of articles about AI, such as "AI and Sci-fi" by Robert A. Sawyer and "Can a Machine Be Conscious?" by Stevan Harnad.

Pew Center on Global Climate Change
2101 Wilson Blvd., Suite 550, Arlington, VA   22201
(703) 516-4146 • fax: (703) 841-1422
website: www.pewclimate.org

The Pew Center on Global Climate Change seeks the cooperation of those working in private industry, government, and scientific fields to address the issues of global warming using science, honesty, and integrity. The center funds research and publications, works directly with policymakers and business leaders to find feasible solutions to climate change problems, and educates the public about their role in slowing global warming. The organization's website provides access to publications on topics ranging from the basics of global warming, to scientific and economic impact, to technological solutions.

Singularity Institute for Artificial Intelligence (SIAI)
PO Box 50182, Palo Alto, CA   94303
phone/fax: (866) 667-2524
e-mail: institute@singinst.org
website: http://singinst.org

SIAI is a nonprofit research institute that aims to develop safe, stable, self-modifying Artificial General Intelligence (AGI), support research into AGI and Friendly AI, and foster the creation of an international research community focused on safe AI. Its website contains articles and links to articles dealing with the impact of advanced AI on humankind's future, many videos of presentations and interviews, and a blog.

US Environmental Protection Agency (EPA)
Ariel Rios Bldg., 1200 Pennsylvania Ave. NW
Washington, DC   20460
(202) 272-0167
website: www.epa.gov

The EPA is the US government agency charged with protecting the environment and the health of US citizens through the development and enforcement of environmental regulations, grant giving, conducting research and publishing studies, and working in partnership with non-governmental organizations. Additionally, the EPA seeks to educate the US public about current environmental issues. The EPA climate change website, www.epa.gov/climatechange, provides the latest information on global warming-related topics such as greenhouse gas emissions, US climate change policy, health and environmental effects, and actions individuals can take to slow global warming. Reports published by the EPA can be accessed online.

Bibliography of Books

Amir D. Aczel   *Present at the Creation: The Story of CERN and the Large Hadron Collider.* New York: Crown, 2010.

Joseph Cirincione   *Bomb Scare: The History and Future of Nuclear Weapons.* New York: Oxford University Press, 2008.

Heidi Cullen   *The Weather of the Future: Heat Waves, Extreme Storms, and Other Scenes from a Climate-Changed Planet.* New York: HarperCollins, 2010.

Tad Daley   *Apocalypse Never: Forging the Path to a Nuclear Weapon-Free World.* Piscataway, NJ: Rutgers University Press, 2010.

Christopher Dodd and Robert Bennett   *The Senate Special Report on Y2K.* Nashville, TN: Thomas Nelson, Inc., 1999.

K. Eric Drexler   *Engines of Creation: The Coming Era of Nanotechnology.* New York: Anchor Books, 1986.

Jean-Pierre Filiu   *Apocalypse in Islam.* Berkeley, CA: University of California Press, 2011.

Bruce David Forbes and Jeanne Halgren Kilde, eds.   *Rapture, Revelation, and the End Times: Exploring the Left Behind Series.* New York: Palgrave MacMillan, 2004.

Lynn E. Foster — *Nanotechnology: Science, Innovation, and Opportunity*. Upper Saddle River, NJ: Prentice Hall, 2009.

John R. Hall, Philip D. Schuyler, and Sylvaine Trinh — *Apocalypse Observed: Religious Movements and Violence in North America, Europe, and Japan*. New York: Routledge, 2000.

Paul Halpern — *The World's Smallest Particles*. Hoboken, NJ: John Wiley & Sons, 2009.

James C. Hansen — *Storms of My Grandchildren: The Truth About the Coming Climate Catastrophe and Our Last Chance to Save Humanity*. New York: Bloomsbury USA, 2009.

John Horgan — *The Undiscovered Mind: How the Human Brain Defies Replication, Medication, and Explanation*. New York: Touchstone, 1999.

Alan Hultberg, ed. — *Three Views on the Rapture: Pretribulation, Prewrath, and Posttribulation*. Grand Rapids, MI: Zondervan, 2010.

Samuel P. Huntington — *The Clash of Civilizations and the Remaking of World Order*. New York: Touchstone, 1996.

John Major Jenkins — *The 2012 Story: The Myths, Fallacies, and Truth Behind the Most Intriguing Date in History*. New York: Penguin Group, 2009.

Jonathan Kirsch   *A History of the End of the World: How the Most Controversial Book in the Bible Changed the Course of History.* New York: HarperCollins, 2006.

Ray Kurzweil   *The Singularity Is Near: When Humans Transcend Biology.* New York: Penguin Group, 2005.

Patrick J. Michaels and Robert Ballins   *Climate of Extremes: Global Warming Science They Don't Want You to Know.* Washington, DC: Cato Institute, 2009.

John Mueller   *Atomic Obsession: Nuclear Alarmism from Hiroshima to Al-Qaeda.* New York: Oxford University Press, 2009.

Sharan Newman   *The Real History of the End of the World: Apocalyptic Predictions from Revelation and Nostradamus to Y2K and 2012.* New York: Berkley Books, 2010.

Kenneth G.C. Newport and Crawford Gribben, eds.   *Expecting the End: Millennialism in Social and Historical Context.* Waco, TX: Baylor University Press, 2006.

Kevin Quigley   *Responding to Crises in the Modern Infrastructure: Policy Lessons from Y2K.* New York: Palgrave Macmillan, 2008.

Bruce Riedel   *The Search for Al Qaeda: Its Leadership, Ideology, and Future*, rev. ed. Washington, DC: Brookings Institution, 2008.

Barbara R. Rossing   *The Rapture Exposed: The Message of Hope in the Book of Revelation*. New York: Basic Books, 2004.

Index